CRITICAL PEACE EDUCATION AND GLOBAL CITIZENSHIP

Critical Peace Education and Global Citizenship offers narrative accounts representing multiple ways teacher and learner activists have come to realize possibilities for peace and reconciliation through unofficial curricula. With these narratives, the book demonstrates the connections between critical peace education and such crucial issues as human trafficking, gang violence, contested narratives of nationhood and belonging, gender identities and the significance of mentoring. Through rich examples of pedagogic work, this volume enhances and illustrates critically oriented understandings and interpretations of peace in real classrooms with diverse populations of students. Written primarily for scholars and graduate students working in the fields of educational theory, critical pedagogy and educational policy, the chapters in this book tell a compelling story about teachers, learners and scholar activists who continue to struggle for the creation of transformative and meaningful sites for peace praxis.

Rita Verma is an Associate Professor in Social Studies Education and Peace Studies at Adelphi University in New York. She collaborates with the UN and various human rights organizations to engage educators in dialogue about human rights and global citizenship.

The Critical Social Thought Series
Edited by Michael W. Apple,
University of Wisconsin–Madison

Critical Perspectives on bell hooks
Maria del Guadalupe Davidson and George Yancy, editors

Advocacy Leadership
Toward a Post-Reform Agenda in Education
Gary L. Anderson

Race, Whiteness, and Education
Zeus Leonardo

Controversy in the Classroom
The Democratic Power of Discussion
Diana E. Hess

The New Political Economy of Urban Education
Neoliberalism, Race, and the Right to the City
Pauline Lipman

Critical Curriculum Studies
Education, Consciousness, and the Politics of Knowing
Wayne Au

Learning to Liberate
Community-Based Solutions to the Crisis in Urban Education
Vajra Watson

Critical Pedagogy and Social Change
Critical Analysis on the Language of Possibility
Seehwa Cho

Educating Activist Allies
Social Justice Pedagogy with the Suburban and Urban Elite
Katy Swalwell

The Political Classroom
Evidence and Ethics in Democratic Education
Diana E. Hess and Paula McAvoy

Mapping Corporate Education Reform
Power and Policy Networks in the Neoliberal State
Wayne Au and Joseph J. Ferrare

The End of Public Schools
The Corporate Reform Agenda to Privatize Education
David Hursh

The Critical Turn in Education
From Marxist Critique to Poststructuralist Feminism to Critical Theories of Race
Isaac Gottesman

CRITICAL PEACE EDUCATION AND GLOBAL CITIZENSHIP

Narratives From the Unofficial Curriculum

Rita Verma

NEW YORK AND LONDON

First published 2017
by Routledge
711 Third Avenue, New York, NY 10017

and by Routledge
2 Park Square, Milton Park, Abingdon, Oxon, OX14 4RN

Routledge is an imprint of the Taylor & Francis Group, an informa business

© 2017 Taylor & Francis

The right of Rita Verma to be identified as author of this work has been asserted by her in accordance with sections 77 and 78 of the Copyright, Designs and Patents Act 1988.

All rights reserved. No part of this book may be reprinted or reproduced or utilised in any form or by any electronic, mechanical, or other means, now known or hereafter invented, including photocopying and recording, or in any information storage or retrieval system, without permission in writing from the publishers.

Trademark notice: Product or corporate names may be trademarks or registered trademarks, and are used only for identification and explanation without intent to infringe.

Library of Congress Cataloging in Publication Data
A catalog record for this book has been requested

ISBN: 978-1-138-64957-6 (hbk)
ISBN: 978-1-138-64956-9 (pbk)
ISBN: 978-1-315-62578-2 (ebk)

Typeset in Bembo
by codeMantra

CONTENTS

Acknowledgements	*vii*
Series Editor Introduction	*ix*

Introduction: Ventures into the Margins: Peace as a Possibility — 1

1 Seeking Peace Activists and Global Citizens — 16

2 The Common Core Reading Program and the Unofficial Lessons on Race: Readings on Roberto Clemente, MLK and Cesar Chavez — 36

3 My Story Our Story: Interpretations of Global Violence and Peace in the Middle School Classroom — 56

4 Dignity for All Students Act and Critical Peace Activism — 64

5 Critical Peace Pedagogues—Shaping Teachers in Training — 78

6 Increase the Peace: A Journey of a Teacher Activist — 101

7 The Story of Soledad: From the Gang Life to Peace Activist — 114

vi Contents

8 Intermittent Interruptions: Patchwork Peace Narratives
From a Human Rights Seminar 126

Conclusion: Now Is the Time to Begin 150

References *161*
Index *167*

ACKNOWLEDGEMENTS

Sometimes it can be the storms and setbacks in our lives that begin to give meaning to our path. It was indeed on a rainy Tuesday afternoon when I began to write down stories, ideas and thoughts that came to mind. Countless dialogues with students, allies and activists that had crossed my path became chronicled on scraps of paper on my desk. It seemed at the time that these scraps were merely mementos for a personal diary or journal. Then the idea for a book came to be.

I am profoundly grateful to Dr. Michael Apple for having the belief and faith in my project and for supporting me through the process. Your encouragement, mentorship and wisdom gave me the fortitude to transform a mere vision and a pile of ideas into a book. I would also like to thank Catherine Bernard and the editorial board at Routledge for your endorsement and support of this project.

This book chronicles the lives of numerous peace activists that continue to be agents of change in our communities. It was a humbling process for me to have the opportunity to highlight the work of my allies. As always, it is my hope that your work is not merely regarded as words on paper, but rather encourages others to follow you and become activists. I want to thank my wonderful students who value the message that I share in my classroom and I admire your endeavors to be greater than yourselves and seek that which is better for your community and the world.

The endless process of writing drafts, rewriting chapters and editing took a village. My dear family and friends understood with patience and love and carried me through the journey. My dear husband Arvinder has always encouraged me to follow my heart and I share my victories, Jaana, with you. The unconditional love of my parents, Mom, Dad and Babaji, and the endearing affection from Parveen, Anand, Meenu and Aiyana are the lifelines for my soul.

viii Acknowledgements

There is one kindred soul for whom I dedicate the entirety of this book and its message. There are few individuals that I know that can inspire me so deeply and incite such wonder inside my heart than my dear son, Armaan. As a young budding poet and writer, I hope you always follow your heart and know that your words can transform lives, as your prose becomes gentle footprints on the lives you touch. Your passion will follow you no matter what path you choose in life.

SERIES EDITOR INTRODUCTION

Although there have been major gains in the struggles toward greater equality throughout the world, we are living in a period of time that is marked by tragedy and human misery. Every day brings us more instances of millions of people fleeing for their lives. Large-scale famine, environmental destruction, mass incarceration, spreading nuclear weaponization, the threats of terrorism, repressive governments, cultural crises and the loss of collective memories and languages, repeated police killings of people of color … the list could go on and on. The accumulation of such things brings with it a familiarity and perhaps even cynicism that must be constantly fought against. These conditions are simply not acceptable.

It also brings with it crucial questions: How are we to understand these events and the processes that underpin them? What prevents us from more critical understanding? What can we as educators do to help prevent such situations and to develop more critical understandings? And finally, who is the "we"? Questions such as these lie at the heart of *Critical Peace Education and Global Citizenship*.

There are of course many groups who are laboring very hard to deny the importance of such questions and who spend large amounts of money in campaigns to convince us that neoliberal and neoconservative agendas are the only "realistic" options that we can dream of and afford in education and so much else (see, e.g., Apple 2006; Mayer 2016; Schirmer and Apple 2016). Yet Verma's narratives remind us that the world is also a place where struggles against this false "realism" can and do go on.

In one of my recent books, I include the story of my experiences in an Asian nation that taught me a good deal about the relationship between international economies and the creation of very damaging inequalities. These experiences

x Series Editor Introduction

had a profound effect on my understanding of the ways in which our daily lives and ordinary commonsense create what might best be called an epistemological fog that covers our invisible but very real participation in a system that leads to the destruction of communities, in large scale forced migration, in the lack of schooling and health care in urban slums and so much else (Davis 2006). In that chapter I trace out the ways in which our love of "cheap French fries" contributes to all of these truly damaging conditions (Apple 2013b).

There have been other instances where these too often hidden (or perhaps the word *ignored* describes this better?) relations have been made very visible to me: in my work on the issues of building critical educational policies and practices in "favelas" in Brazil; in my efforts in nations that have been torn apart by civil wars and wars of imperialism; in supporting activist groups that are building schools for the children of migrant populations who are struggling for a better life for their children.

Or I could go back even further: to the time I spent as a youth worker in the extremely poor sections of the city in New Jersey where I was born; and to my participation in anti-racist movements and organizations even when I was still a teenager.

My point in noting all of these things is not to highlight myself as in any way special. I am certain that many of the readers of Rita Verma's fine and honest book will have themselves done similar things and more at many levels of society—and are continuing to do so. Rather, it is to the credit of the book you are about to read that it brings back an entire array of personal memories of why the issue of peace is so important and why we need to expand our justifiable concern for peace into areas that may not be as cogently dealt with in the existing literature.

Critical Peace Education and Global Citizenship demonstrates the connections between peace education and such crucial issues as sex trafficking, gang violence, gender and people's identities, the significance of mentoring and similar things. At the same time, it provides rich examples of pedagogic work on enhancing critically oriented understandings and actions on peace in real classrooms with diverse populations of students. But it doesn't end there. Verma gives us accounts of very interesting work on peace and global citizenship with future teachers as well as with the wider population of undergraduates at colleges and universities.

This is not a disembodied book. Rita Verma enables us to see the realities of peace and its absence through her own eyes. Thus she is fully present—as a practicing critical teacher and teacher educator. But we also are given space to see the word through the eyes of those who all too often are nameless and faceless, who live in the places and relations that remain unseen in the conditions of the dominant epistemological fog. In so doing, *Critical Peace Education and Global Citizenship* plays another important role.

In *Can Education Change Society?* (Apple 2013a), I detail a number of tasks that the critical scholar/activist should perform. Among these are:

1 "Bearing witness to negativity". That is, telling the truth about the realities and inequalities of this society.
2 Illuminating spaces for possible actions that can challenge these realities.
3 Acting as the "critical secretary" of the people, programs and practices that are actually interrupting dominant relations and building workable alternatives to them in educational institutions, communities and other sites.

Verma takes all three of these tasks seriously and does them in what are often compelling ways. The story with which she begins simply grabs the reader. It involves sex-trafficking "menus", where sex tourism gives the "customer" a choice among children whose bodies are for sale. This is an example that makes us confront the human (and inhumane) costs to real people of this practice in our society and so many others. Her discussion of what then happened in her own classroom when she dealt honestly with such practices demonstrates the pedagogic possibilities of challenging the epistemological fog. And this is not the only time when Rita Verma points to real educational possibilities both inside and outside of schools.

While there is a rich tradition of thoughtful literature in peace education, the breadth and depth of this book is rare in the literature on peace education. This by itself would make for a very useful volume. But when one adds the fact that it is conceptually rich and creatively draws upon analyses in critical pedagogy, critical race theory and critical studies of globalization and citizenship as well, its value is increased.

There's an old saying from social movements involved in peace that goes like this: "Peace starts with me". Rita Verma helps point to ways where this journey can begin.

Michael W. Apple
John Bascom Professor of
Curriculum and Instruction
and
Educational Policy Studies
University of Wisconsin–Madison

References

Apple, M. W. (2006). *Educating the "Right" Way: Markets, Standards, God, and Inequality* (2nd edition). New York: Routledge.
Apple, M. W. (2013a). *Can Education Change Society?* New York: Routledge.

xii Series Editor Introduction

Apple, M. W. (2013b). *Knowledge, Power, and Education*. New York: Routledge.

Davis, M. (2006). *Planet of Slums*. New York: Verso.

Mayer, J. (2016). *Dark Money: The Hidden History of the Billionaires Behind the Rise of the Radical Right*. New York: Doubleday.

Schirmer, E. and Apple, M. W. (2016). Capital, Power, and Education: "Dark Money" and the Politics of Common-Sense. *Education Review*, 23 (September 28). http://dx.doi.org/10.14507/er.v23.2145.

INTRODUCTION

Ventures into the Margins: Peace as a Possibility

The "Menu"

The menu was handed to the student in the first row. With her eyes downcast, refusing to look, she slid the menu face down to the student next to her. The male student peered down and looked away exhibiting a sense of discomfort. The menu was passed amongst the students, incurring various responses. I looked up and watched as a few students wiped tears away from their eyes while some others exhibited a nervous laugh. We had entered a hidden and raw space of violation and a sexually violent space of dehumanization; we were "bearing witness" to the commodification of children's bodies. The menu, a tattered makeshift display, presented images of young girls and boys alongside sexual acts and services. Children as young as 5 and 6 years old were on display for purchase. Following each image was a shoddily handwritten price related to each act presenting a myriad of choices for the customer. Prices shifted in order of "value" of the young child, younger being more expensive and older less so. The youngest victims were the highest valued "commodity" and oftentimes purchasing and deflowering one was regarded as a good luck omen for businessmen. As an order at a restaurant, the lives of these children were minimized to being mere commodities with a price. A rarely discussed artifact of the sex trade and global human trafficking was staring us in the face.

The story of this menu, however, is more profound. Upon her travels as an activist and abolitionist in Southeast Asia this menu had been presented to our guest speaker, Sue Lingenfelter from Love146. Love146 is an international anti-trafficking organization that was co-founded by Rob Morris in the year 2002. Along with fellow activists, Sue described how they were preyed upon as potential customers due to being "Western" as global sex tourism is a lucrative business for the locals. Sex tourists travel to other countries and are individuals

2 Introduction

who solicit and buy commercial sex and are able to do so due to weak legal systems. These systems turn a blind eye to the exploitation of girls, especially those from poor and marginalized communities. Between illegal drugs and arms trafficking, global sex tourism is a $32 billion industry. Eighty percent of trafficked victims are abused as sexual slaves. The street where they were handed the menu was a flea market where locals purchased their daily staple of food and on the other side of the street the sex market was on display with neon lighting, English music and sex peddlers. As undercover human rights activists they were educating themselves on these brothels and sex shops. Sue was only witness to the realities outside of the brothels and held back tears as she described older girls (the younger ones were hidden away until they were bought) and boys being put on sale and on display in plain sight for all to see. In a previous trip, Rob Morris had entered the brothel in order to understand the horrors that victims endured in the shadows of society. Once inside the brothel Rob Morris stood shoulder to shoulder with predators as girls were on display behind a glass windowpane with numbers on their dresses. These little girls were forever being enslaved by a debt they were told they owed the pimps and hence would be forced to entertain up to 50 customers a day. Girls who refused were beaten unconscious, electrocuted and cut. The dehumanization of these children to mere numbers made them nameless and faceless victims. Sue Lingenfelter would later tell the class that the number 146 represented a number that was pinned on a little girls dress. Rob Morris had noticed that amongst the girls in the room waiting to be purchased while watching cartoons, the girl with the number 146 stared out at the predators and was described as having a fight left in her eyes. The fate of the little girl with the number 146 is not known. And hence Love146 is symbolic in the organizations' purpose to continue her fight–to abolish the global sex trade of children and restore dignity to these young victims.

Classroom seats creaked and shifted and silence ensued as the level of discomfort in the room engulfed us. Treading upon a deeply personal and conflictual space, an opening was realized. Perhaps in their lifetimes, students were the closest they might ever be to the realities and darkness of child trafficking. Now that we had pried the lever open and had been confronted on profound personal and political levels, the pedagogical space in the room was unchartered territory. Who would speak first and respond to what they had just seen? As a class we were suddenly pushed into bearing a shared responsibility for the dehumanization of these children. This was the truth. The silence in the room for me symbolized an ideological confrontation. Students were challenged to face the dark spaces where the West meets the developing world, where privilege and power corrupt and victimize the vulnerable, where patriarchal forms disavow the rights of children and women and where assumptions about "peace" are in fact feigned ignorance about everyday violence. We are awakened to the fact that we live our lives impervious to these dark realities. Our privilege stared us back in the face and created an opening that was interruptive.

Engagement with the menu exposed vulnerabilities and assumptions and simultaneously triggered hopelessness and helplessness in the face of dire exploitation. It cut at the heart of assumptions about peace, human rights and global citizenship and ultimately the frameworks of peace education would be recast in meaningful ways as these contextualized openings were created. The engagement with commodified bodies became the basis of the lens we were crafting to understand peace. In our classroom, the frameworks of peace praxis would only take on real meaning when "peace" or the absence of it was understood in the contextualization of real lives and trauma. Our shared responsibility, confrontations and revelations about dehumanization in our daily thoughts and practices, systems and interactions were "fair game" in our critical pedagogical space. It is within these unchartered frameworks that pedagogue and learner are able to "hear" and "reveal" their authentic selves and mutually share and explore the possibilities, it is where learners can reveal, that I'm upset; I'm traumatized; I'm hurting; I was raped; I feel helpless and I want to make a difference. It is where we can mutually question our compliance with oppression and objectification of the "Other" and relate our understandings of what the possibilities of peace can be.

The journey of every teacher is filled with moments of struggle, disillusionment and contemplation and is essentially a winding road with roadblocks, obstructed pathways and landscapes under construction. As someone who is acutely aware and is in constant evaluation of the social, political and economic forces that shape us, I view my classroom as a space to explore them. There are some key moments I will share from my unfinished journey to understand what it meant to "teach peace" and to hone opportunities to teach peace. My classroom experiences began in both urban and suburban public school systems. Both settings, as are all pedagogical spaces, were platforms to explore facets of peace education. Within my own struggles to grasp its meanings in various contexts, there was an ongoing need to recast meanings and understandings of peace or the possibilities of peace. As a new teacher in both school settings I had my own deep sense of discomfort, yet felt compelled to position my classroom within symbolically violent contexts to pose counter narratives. The establishment of No Child Left Behind and the terrorist attacks of 9/11 framed the socio-political contexts of the beginnings of my teaching experience in New York. Now to begin, I believed it was important to develop an identity of a teacher activist and to have confidence that being a teacher activist was legitimate and empowering. Within the larger crowd of teachers who did not share my ideas, what would it mean to be radical and counterhegemonic?

"I Refuse"

Within an ethnic enclave of predominately African American, Haitian and West Indian immigrant students, I taught in an urban school setting in Brooklyn, New York 15 years ago. The school had a high turnover rate in

4 Introduction

school leadership, had outdated books and was a building infested with rats and mice where bathrooms were padlocked shut, and overcrowding contributed to the challenges. With over 1200 students in the building, 90 percent received free and reduced lunch, one in four students had a learning disability and the teaching staff had classroom sizes with upwards of 40 students. The neighborhood was marred with violence and poverty and gangs frequently recruited near schools. It was blatantly unfair to students and teachers as systemic violence, inequality and racism had written these students off from society. Students were confronted by the unwritten message that society had in many ways turned its backs on their struggles. There was a daily trial to survive for my students and making it into the school doors in the morning was a victory in itself.

During the school day, fights would break out in the hallways, there was drinking and smoking in the stairwells and there were few students who engaged in the curriculum. Every school day, I would travel between six different classrooms because I did not have a home base. Carrying my notes on large sketchpad paper, I carried my curriculum throughout the building and attempted to be as effective as possible. I understood the students struggled with the material, as their thoughts were elsewhere. Fellow teachers reminded me of the need to create a highly militaristic command of the class with tightly aligned classroom rows with not a sound to be heard by students. The classroom was supposed to have a monotonous daily routine where I teach, they listen and we get through the lesson and move on to the next. The year I began teaching here, biannual testing for the NAEP Trial Urban District Assessment (TUDA) began. The school district would now be required to submit data to determine adequate yearly progress. Given my understanding of the school setting and the daily struggles of the students it was clear to me that the school would be in danger of being labeled "failing". Students carried within them profound injuries of race and class. As victims of injuries of race and class, my students were clearly the oppressed. They understood well, on a daily basis, that they were expected to fail and their very lives were in need of a counter narrative or a buffer to the messages that society was telling them.

Trying to realize tightly aligned rows and a room full of quiet obedient students was an uphill battle. I began to doubt my own abilities as an educator and was told by fellow staff that I needed to assert authority and presence with a no nonsense kind of attitude. This expectation contradicted my vision and perspectives about teaching and learning and it was difficult to model my classroom after the militaristic authoritarian framework. After several weeks of failing to adhere to rigor and authority, I decided to tailor my classroom to what I believed would elicit learning and growth. My classroom did not have straight rows nor was it silent. In fact, it would become a room full of conversation and laughter. Collaboration and cooperative modes of learning replaced competitive learning, which is a hallmark of peace education. Students worked better in collaboration, through dialogue and discussion and through collectively solving problems. When students entered my classroom they were allowed to pick their seats, allowed to work with one another and encouraged to speak. The background hum of the broken radiator was overtaken by a selection of students' favorite music. Through this collaborative classroom model I began to connect with my students. It was on a daily basis that I would notice the student in class that had shut down emotionally or mentally to the task at hand. There was anger and frustration that would erupt in the room.

In particular one student named Javari, a 16-year-old student who was held back in the 8th grade, would challenge me. In quiet, honest ways Javari would ask me about my life and my struggle. He would ask how I could possibly relate to them. Javari would expose the elephant in the room, which was the lack of trust that had enveloped the community for long. It was indeed the lack of trust in their lives and future by schools and society and the students' wariness and distrustfulness in an educator that refused to abandon and fail them. They had every reason to distrust me and I acknowledged that within myself. There were many days when the lesson plan book never was cracked open and instead I initiated conversations and interactions. Is there anything that I can help you with? Are you okay? Are you hurting? Is anger the solution? Will it help to sing or dance to express your feelings? Through the school year, I developed an intimate understanding of the lives of my students because their struggles and challenges were relevant and important to me. For my students "bearing witness" to oppression was counterintuitive, since they themselves were immersed in oppressive ideological forms. They were the victims of gentrification, white flight, poverty, violence and racism. It was I who was the student in the room, or "bearing witness", as I came to understand the difficulties of survival in the urban landscape and the very real dangers they faced on a daily basis. In the Freiran sense, "through dialogue the teacher-of-the-students and the students-of-the-teacher cease to exist and new term emerges-teacher-student with student-teachers". In my classroom, both teacher and student were simultaneously occupying both roles. As much as they struggled, there was a sense of pride in their ethnicity, their neighborhoods and the sense of ownership of their school. It was far from perfect and I had no intention of feigning a "victim-savior" relationship to them. Frameworks of peace education took on meaning as students began to sense a safe space in my classroom. As students began to critically understand their embeddedness in structures of power that were symbolically violent on many levels, the openings for dialogue were realized. Until students themselves developed a sense of purpose or imagining, the daily curriculum held little meaning. In the classroom, I began to occupy a mutual lens of both teacher activist and peace educator. As an activist, I became an advocate for my students and their needs and as a peace educator I sought to engage them in alternative viewpoints and dialogue in regard to their response to violence and dehumanization.

6 Introduction

At the end of the school year, there was a moment of confrontation that would in essence become a peaceful protest. When I entered the school building it was eerily quiet. Students walked the halls with their heads turned down. It was the day of an 8th grade standardized assessment test, which was the required test for the NAEP. Perhaps it was the nervousness or pressure to perform in order to not be labeled a failing school that triggered the unsettling silence. This would be another example of systemic violence within the school in the face of the complicated struggles the students faced on a daily basis. There was, however, a more serious reason. Javari had completed all required work and was on his way to graduate from middle school. This was the celebration we hoped to have. Reality, however, wrote a different ending to the story. Caught between gang rivalry, as a bystander on a street corner, Javari had been gunned down and killed the night before. I was overcome by deep sadness, anger, frustration, defeat and hopelessness all at once and was hit by the stark reminder that realized peace within schools is in sharp contrast to the violent streets. The agenda of the school day was enforced by the building administration. Similar to the manner in which society erases the humanity of disadvantaged youth, they were expected to turn off their emotional switch and sit down and take a standardized test. Javari, a soon to be adult in an 8th grade classroom, had been failed by the system and further, his premature death was symbolic of the countless lives lost to complicated forms of violence and youth gang rivalry. Essentially in this moment of mourning for my students, their needs to console one another, their emotional distress and their need to engage in solace was stripped from them as the task of the day held precedence. Sit down, take the test and deal with your feelings later. It was the most dehumanizing moment of the school year. It symbolized the many ways violent forms occupied their lives.

This moment elucidated the manner the overt violence of gun violence confronts the covert violence of schools that don't care and educational agendas that minimize their identities to mere numbers. It was a moment that I felt deeply compelled to interrupt. On that solemn day to honor the memory of Javari, the class sat in my room in a circle of remembrance. There was grieving, laughter and tears. It was symbolic in that the loss of Javari and their lives were dignified. It became the "unofficial" curriculum of the day. In our resistance and engagement with this counterhegemonic act, a moment of transformation was realized and as their teacher, "teaching peace" only found a meaningful context when their lives mattered. The pile of tests lay abandoned on my desk, unopened and unadministered. The door to our classroom remained shut and this symbolized our resistance to the "education" machine that intended to further violate and minimize these students' lives to mere quantifiable objects. This peaceful protest characterized by deeply meaningful actions to interrupt complicated and violent hegemonic forms illuminates how an unofficial "peace education" curriculum transpired.

9/11: Essential Disruptions

Shifting within situational contexts, peace education as a tool to interrupt hegemonic forms took on a different meaning in a suburban affluent community. On the heels of 9/11, within the complicated political climate of fear and terrorism, schools were challenged to handle the event in a variety of ways. Albeit, a sense of discomfort and reluctance shaped the complicated engagement with global events and with due respect to lives lost and families that were intimately impacted by the tragic day, the manner this particular school chose to memorialize 9/11 became a point of departure to teach peace. The spawning of racist nativist forms after 9/11 were intimately tied to my own identity and community. Fellow Sikh colleagues, friends and family were being assaulted and racially profiled. Lives were becoming defined by fear and helplessness as places of worship and neighborhoods witnessed defacing, violence and hate. There was little interruption by the news media and schools and the victims of the war on terror were not only innocent civilians across the world and in the Middle East, they were now also neighbors and community members. It became essential to disrupt and educate the general public on cultural practices and histories of the Sikh community. In solidarity, the Muslim community also had to engage in a tremendous amount of grassroots work in order to undo and disrupt Islamophobia. Organizations such as the Sikh Coalition and the Arab-American Anti-Discrimination Committee took on the charge to document hate crimes and educate the public about their communities. In my previous work, *Dialogues about 9/11 Media and Race: Lessons from a Secondary Classroom* in *Radical Teacher* (2005), I documented in-depth the lessons that took place in my classroom related to disrupting racist nativist, xenophobic and Islamophobic forms.

In this particular school, the memorialization of terrorism through patriotic displays and inadvertent correlations of turbaned bearded men with fear was unfair as the events were masked by curriculums that reproduced ideological forms that were overtly violent. Students were being targeted in the hallway and called "terrorist". Harmful jokes were casually asserted and these acts were discriminating and profiling groups. My classroom space was transformed into a critical site to deconstruct and analyze growing stereotypes and assumptions about people, places and things that were being "Othered" as the enemy. The dialogue that was created in my classroom went against the general attitudes in the building. In my language classroom, the week allotted for fun cultural activities and food tasting was replaced with serious discourse about the dangers of stereotyping through self-reflection activities about social attitudes and racism. Media analysis and tackling the presence of ideological forms formed the basis to understand the political climate and social repercussions being felt in the community. Mutually engaging in dialogues about "hate" allowed students to realize how oppression touched all of our lives. This experience

8 Introduction

illustrates yet another approach to "peace education" as being defined by relational encounters, interruptive action and meaning making in the context of the moment and through lived experiences.

Seeking Peace Education

Gathering from my past experiences, I have understood that schools most often are unlikely places where peace education practices can lead to systemic transformation. In many ways disrupting the nature of educational systems and its contradictory forms becomes the insurmountable task. Education in itself is a form of indoctrination and "peace" remains an undefined term. Together that leaves us with "indoctrination" into the "undefined" and is problematic. The open-endedness in defining peace can be a double-edged sword. On the one hand, students are empowered to continually define and redefine peace in meaningful and engaged dialogue and hence create radical openings. On the other hand, the imagined moral code of right and wrong is a blurred landscape and achieving "peace" in the world is correlated with engaging violence. To preserve "global peace", violence is employed in the guise of democracy. To realize "peace in the streets", mass unnecessary incarcerations take place. To preserve "morality and peace", groups of people are admonished with homophobia. To foster "peaceful schools" for children, segregation takes place to ensure one's children do not attend schools with the perceived dangerous "Other". The knowledge within us about the social order is symbolically violent and reproduced with little interruption. Such troubled knowledge and normalized ideas about violent "peace" when confronted do not necessarily become de-stabilized. Confrontations do not necessarily lead to transformation in many instances because students themselves possess a gaze that is deeply embedded in privilege. This resistance is emblematic of privilege, apathy, detachment, and isolationism in our neighborhoods, communities and nation-states. Acquiring peace knowledge rarely results in peace activism due to apathy, privilege and the normalization of violence and the dehumanization in society becomes a constant reminder of our entrenchment within hegemonic forms.

The vision of this book builds on the current work of peace educators and researchers in the field and will further debunk the understanding that "peace education" is a linear process of acquiring subject matter knowledge from a set of defined packaged curriculum content. Narratives in this book represent multiple ways teacher activists and learner activists have come to know or understand possibilities for peace and reconciliation in unofficial ways. These narratives recast the notion that peace and global citizenship are quantifiable end "products" of a perceived curriculum pathway. These stories of "activists at work" also inspire us to act despite the daunting violence and global crises that surround us. The current frameworks that shape teachers demand a com-partmentalization of their work. Due to the nature of this, teachers and schools function within agendas that are deeply in conflict with contested identities and pedagogies of critical peace education and global citizenship. Pedagogies of resistance and reconciliation, for example, are viewed as corrosive to the "perceived" normalcy of the school day and are oftentimes silenced.

Schools continue to function within structures of passive compliance and obedience and are factory lines producing uncritical and passive students. As beacons of transformation and possibility, schools are in many ways burdened with conformity. Schools today serve as the primary filtering mechanism in society stressing competition while simultaneously aggrandizing rhetoric of cooperative and collective learning. "Cooperative learning" is oftentimes packaged in a peace curriculum that produces superficial and oversimplified engagements with no long lasting impact. John Dewey (1916) argued that schooling was central in teaching children modes of associated living and social interaction. Many progressive goals that once dominated public education debates that shared frameworks of peace education including inculcation of critical thinking and political literacy, fostering of self-esteem and self-actualization, cultivation of creativity and development of caring and tolerant citizens have been replaced by the economic imperatives of industry and global competitiveness (Torres et al. 2006 p. 6). Failed policies and reforms around "undoing" oppression of the poor, the illiterate and silenced communities around us have inevitably lead to greater resistance and struggle. Testing, teacher accountability and student achievement have become the defining points of discussions when understanding the purpose and value of public schools. The labor of teachers has become a data driven regiment and their work has become limited to pre-defined parameters.

I think it is important to raise the following question, that within the existing limitations of curriculum frameworks, can unofficial curriculums become transformative sites for peace praxis? Let's take a step back for a moment. Paolo Freire rejected agendas to convert his educational philosophy into formalized classroom activity handbooks. Freire argued rather that individual situations demanded unique liberation practices and contexts and cataloguing critical pedagogy would be counterintuitive. According to Freire, a critical pedagogy "must be made and remade" (1997 p. 30). In a similar vein, peace education is in constant redefinition and its' meaning critically recast in relation to contexts that are authentic to the moment. Freire's powerful insight allows us to understand that contrary to the common practice of compartmentalizing peace education as packaged content, "teaching" peace is often confrontational and unpredictable as well. Disrupting an uncritical "official" curriculum and transforming it to become critical peace education in the unofficial space can be political and radical work.

Reflecting upon teaching in the classroom on the heels of 9/11 and then today as we experience deeply disturbing violent events of terrorism, racist nativism and homophobia, my identity as a scholar-teacher-activist remain

10 Introduction

unfinished. If I were to hand you a guide and a step-by-step process, and profess that given the right curriculum it will be peace education, it would remain rhetorical. And more often than not, the realization of critical peace activism or humanization will be absent from such packaged curriculum. And now you may ask why? To be quite honest, the reason why may be as simple as the dependence on viewing learning as a quantifiable end result of the accumulation of products. As consumers of knowledge, we accumulate what is to be known. It becomes a means to an end, whereas issues such as peace, human rights and activism are a means to a beginning. This beginning can be described as a place that is radical, political and deeply engaged and where teachers and learners craft counter narratives and forge renewed meaning and solutions to transform themselves and others.

Critical peace education should ideally disrupt normalized everyday thinking where violent forms in "common sense" are interrogated. When each individual recognizes that we collectively participate in violence and bear the responsibility to transform it, perhaps change is possible. The legitimization of identities, histories and voices is meaningful and is necessary because it is not until we ourselves can imagine or connect with stories and lives that we can find or give meaning or value to these dialogues and begin to define peace. Perhaps peace praxis and political projects may only take on real meaning when the act of destabilizing ideologies incites learners to want to know more rather than resist the disruption. Whether that means localized classroom role-plays where students discover activism within themselves or actually standing on the front lines to protest against Boko Haram in Chibok, Nigeria, it is meaningful work. Regardless of the student body it always becomes a unique pedagogical space tailored to the bodies and ideological frameworks in the room. Frameworks of peace education shift depending on the context of the pedagogical space where ideological frameworks are potentially destabilized and imagined possibilities for peace and solutions to violence also remain within continuous redefinition. The pedagogue must see oneself as unfinished and in constant negotiation with the meaning of peace praxis; hence we experience it's making and remaking.

I hope to repeatedly illustrate in this book that as we expose intersectionalities between historical memory, human suffering and lived experiences, peace praxis may become engaged and hence we begin to grapple with "peace". Critical peace education in many ways is a struggle over contested "identities", symbolic violence and its meaning as well as shared ownership of the pedagogical space. When students "bear witness" and make truths relevant, acknowledge privilege and make the raw brutality of human rights violations known, the openings are created. Openings are created when unlimited questioning is encouraged of the past, present and future and when the three are understood to be in continual embrace and tension. To what limits might we be destined if we were to engage in a constant ongoing awareness and engagement with the overt and covert symbolic violence where we are all participants? The stories I share in this book collectively represent the smallest cracks cast upon the greater ideological wall of everyday violence and human suffering. Mobilizations around issues of violence and injustice keep the conversation alive and together they form collective alliances. Building upon the work of critical peace educators, I hope to espouse the tensions and "possibilities for peace" that are developed within the limitations of everyday curriculums. It is with these ideas that I hope you will continue to read further and explore many more examples of teacher activists and *learner-actors* engaged in transformative dialogues and interruptive politics to constantly redefine the parameters of critical peace pedagogy.

Landscape of the Book

In order to conceptualize the moments or "openings" where critical peace education transpires, I would like to take the reader on a journey across diverse pedagogical sites. Narratives in this book illustrate the process by which critical spaces are realized for learner and teacher alike. The stories that are documented in this book did not form part of a short-term study, but rather represent a collection of vignettes that have been gathered throughout many years. Stemming from my own personal life-long inquiry into the manner "peace education" is understood in schools and communities, I have crossed paths with many scholars, teachers and activists. As critical action researchers, their narratives of reflection and self-study will be illuminated. Collectively, these chapters tell a story about teachers, learners and scholar activists who struggle to define "peace" praxis. It is within the struggle to define and know peace that radical understandings take place. A common thread that connects the chapters is the "critical" work that individuals are doing. These critical scholars, teachers and activists embody aspects of Michael Apple's framework on critical scholars that is outlined in the book, *Can Education Change Society?* (2013). Namely, Apple reminds us that the act of becoming a critical scholar/ activist is a complex one and is in constant definition and further he outlines nine tasks that must take place in education for critical analysis (Apple 2013 p. 42). Michael Apple makes the strong argument that educators must "engage with the responsibilities of being scholar/activists, of being organic public intellectuals" (p. 146) and actively participate in efforts that challenge dominant and oppressive systems of authority. Apple also reminds us that "no place is too small, no policy too insignificant, that it can't be the site of challenges" (p. 149).

As we journey into the intimate classroom and community spaces of these individuals, we begin to understand the unique processes that can unfold when deconstructing and understanding that violence is germane, and possibilities for peace take on real meaning. Beyond research, the day-to-day realities and struggles and classroom examples of "activist" work will be highlighted. As a former teacher and a current teacher educator, narratives will be drawn from

12 Introduction

the community, elementary and secondary school setting as well as the college level classroom. Through the lessons learned in this book, the "unofficial curriculum" of critical self-reflection could perhaps become more standardized in the pursuit of educating for democracy and dehumanization. The realm of possibility on the margins is where many teachers and community activists reside and practice their everyday pedagogy and become the moral compass for students. Matters of dignity resound profoundly for these individuals as they bring to life "critical ways of being". The countless examples will illuminate how peace praxis is "made and remade". Through personal narratives, teacher and student voices as well as curricular analysis, unofficial curriculum spaces will be portrayed. I would like to now describe briefly the chapters in this book.

In order to situate many of the narratives in the book, a sound theoretical understanding is crucial. In Chapter 1, theories and research related to critical peace education and global citizenship will be explored. Various arguments will be highlighted that resonate with the arguments in this book as well. Most importantly, I explore what the possibilities can be in order to engage in meaningful peace praxis on the margins of official curriculum frameworks. With the theoretical frameworks as a harness, I will further develop my focus on schools and teacher practice as related to peace.

Action research is defined as a process of systematic inquiry that aims to improve social issues affecting the lives of everyday people. In this case, action research was dynamic and cyclical and I document these repeated cycles of planning, observing and reflecting insights by critical peace education practices. As an action researcher, I will provide an in-depth understanding of pedagogical practices and student voices as well as teacher reflection. The teachers that share their work are also action researchers. Chapter 2 will address the "compromises" on curriculum where students are now exposed to more diverse curriculum under the guise of the common core benchmarks. Although the common core curriculum has sparked off a hotly contested national debate, teachers are coupling common core knowledge with deeply radical and meaningful discussions. Based on an analysis of a local school district and ELA readings administered during the 2014–2015 school year, an analysis will be presented about the diverse reading content, lessons and student responses. Teacher activists, who are also peace educators, move the classroom dialogue beyond the scripted curriculum to create unique pedagogical spaces to create the openings about sensitive topics to create possibilities for peace. In this chapter, elementary students develop collective activists projects to address segregation and racism in their local schools and communities. Moving on to the junior high school years, Chapter 3 will further highlight the work of a middle school teacher that engages their students in powerful conversations about the cyclical nature of violence in our societies. Using the last half hour of the school day, the teacher and students take ownership of the classroom space to engage in these serious debates apart from the official

Introduction **13**

agenda of the day. Using historical imagery and empathy as a prompt, the students in the classroom are given the charge to reflect, imagine and transplant images of the past to the present moment. Through these classroom practices, students are provided with a powerful lens from which to understand and connect the past and present as well as the local and the global. The openings for radical work are created when students are then empowered to imagine solutions to interrupt cycles of violence and discover solutions within themselves and one another. In Chapter 4, the conversation in the book will turn to school climate and bullying.

School climate becomes a central issue that hinders certain student populations from full engagement with their educational experiences. Although elementary students in Chapter 2 addressed issues of school climate in their classrooms, Chapter 4 will look statewide and critique aspects of the Dignity for All Students Act in New York that addresses bullying and student safety in public schools. School climate plays a key role in student well-being and I explore the powerful lesson that elucidate how one moment of bullying can lead to a genocide. In this chapter the DASA act of 2012 in NY State will be analyzed to understand its impact on local school districts on issues related to bullying harassment and discrimination. Programs from two local organizations, the Holocaust Memorial and Tolerance Center and AJK Diversified, will be highlighted and their impact and work in local school districts will be analyzed. Understanding how the work of these two organizations directly relates to building peaceful school climates will be important. Ultimately, teachers are the focus of this book and given the fact that peace education is rarely a defined component of teacher training, I will then venture into my own classroom with pre-service teachers.

In Chapter 5, I invite the reader into my classroom. I ask the important question that as a scholar activist. What role can I embrace in preparing future educators to engage in critical peace pedagogy? Teacher educators play a special role in helping to foster self-reflection and awareness of oppression for teacher candidates in their programs. Through numerous activities and discussions, my teacher education class will be highlighted to illustrate where such discussions are possible and can lead to a sense of empowerment and enlightenment for teacher education candidates. Teacher candidates become exposed to peace education practices and further are challenged to embrace peace praxis in their future teaching careers. Throughout my years as a faculty member, I have had the honor of meeting teacher activists who are deeply involved in political projects and peace activism. In particular, one educator stands out in my mind. Sharing their journey as a teacher activist and peace advocate, the challenges they faced will be elucidated. Chapter 6 will explore the story of one educator's life journey of teaching peace in the late 1960s to the current day. Following the intimate understanding of this teacher activist, I will also share the story of a learner activist who transformed their life of violence.

14 Introduction

Chapter 7 will highlight the survival of a young Latina woman who was born into the gang life and was also a former gang member surviving the injuries of race and class. Such populations are extremely difficult to penetrate and embrace as local school districts fail to understand their needs. Through the work of local community activists, the journey of this young Latina gang survivor will be illustrated. Her life will also be paralleled to work done locally by activists and social workers that work closely with the Latino gang population. The final chapter in this book will move to a broader understanding of how critical peace education can be developed in general education classrooms. Aside from future teachers, future individuals in society in all fields can benefit from critical engagement with the world. Chapter 8 will take place in my classroom in a human rights seminar. Young adults can be the future trendsetters and change agents of our communities. What does it mean when issues of human rights, and global responsibility are incorporated into the curriculum? This chapter will highlight one freshman seminar that included a very diverse group of students from different parts of the world. Coming together, individuals in the class transformed themselves and one another.

At every page turned of the newspaper, I observe multiple forms of violence. Terrorism in Nice, France, airport bombings in Istanbul, Turkey and Belgium, car bombings in Baghdad, police brutality and racial profiling, human trafficking, abject poverty and global illiteracy and the largest massacre in history at a gay club in Orlando, Florida provide a weekly glimpse of the state of world. Daily we also face constant reminders of institutionalized racism and sexism that act in symbolically violent ways to shut out countless individuals in society. The slow escalation of terrorist attacks, police brutality, homophobic, sexist and xenophobic mobilizations are shaping a generation that is seemingly failing to interrupt and interrogate these realities. And the need to disrupt ideological and symbolic forms of violence seems more pressing than ever. Overwhelming feelings of frustration and helplessness for teachers are real, yet as we form radical collective movements, we cannot succumb to defeat. Although I do not have the answers, I am candid about my understanding that deeply meaningful and political projects do indeed exist and deserve notice. Although teaching during times of crisis and global violent uprisings situates educators within complicated terrains, Maxine Greene (2005) reminded us that these crises could be transformed to become possibilities. She probed the reader with the following questions:

> How do we deal with the crumbling of the taken-for-granted, of the reliable, and predictable? How do we justify our own privilege, the privilege of being spared? And how, perhaps most fundamentally of all, do we move the young to reach beyond themselves for the sake of their future and the community-in-the-making we call democracy?
>
> (2005 p. 77)

Greene further extrapolated on the choice teachers have to either garner "safe" spaces that are shut off from the world in the classroom or to generate a "passion for the possible" for our students. It is imperative that students take "ownership" of their interpretations of these crises in order to nurture authentic dialogue. When we choose to navigate the terrain of the "possible", the "otherwise" and the "what if", we reject complacency. When contradictory forms are grappled with, we willingly invite discomfort and the unknown and understand that the direction we seek requires student collaboration and critical dialogue. With these important thoughts in mind, situating "critical peace praxis" within everyday pedagogy also becomes a choice. Imagining what "peace" is in the face of violence and global crises remains undefined, yet let us begin somewhere and understand the ideas that have historically shaped the concepts of peace, peace education and global citizenship in Chapter 1.

1
SEEKING PEACE ACTIVISTS AND GLOBAL CITIZENS

A Difficult Landscape to Tread

> Our language, our behavior, our relationships, our attitudes, in short almost everything about the human being is now conditioned by the "culture of violence". If we achieve peace through war—It is a peace of the graveyard.
> Arun Gandhi

The world is anything but "peaceful" in any given historic timeframe. Peace, in itself, remains an openly contested abstract notion and as I have previously argued, it remains largely undefined. Efforts to realize peace can quickly lead to stagnation and frustration as at any one moment we are immersed in multiple contradictory violent forms and tensions. Faith in peace building and peace-keeping missions remains largely contested as the United Nations, although they may have good intentions, does not possess the force of law in the face of sovereign state bodies. A snapshot of life during World War II with mass geno-cide, the internment of "feared" groups and the hierarchies of gender, peoples and races could be easily paralleled to life in the present moment as the war drums beat alongside rhetoric of exclusion and profiling of populations. The re-jection of nation-states to open borders to the mass migration of Syrian refugees can also be likened to the plight of Jewish refugees during the Holocaust era.

The idea of "global citizenship" faces similar challenges as well in terms of the realization of participatory, equal and just human relations and uni-versal access to power. The posturing of liberal democracies, dialogue about borders and the preservation of "nationhood" symbolize how deeply divided human civil society remains to be. Benhabib (2004) rightly states that, "we have to learn to live with the otherness of Others whose way of being may be deeply threatening to our own" (p. 60). Nation states, however, are deeply entrenched in policies that exclude, demand assimilation and further outright ban traditions and customs that appear "endangering" to romanticized notions of what it means to belong in nation-states. The success of the Brexit initiative, or the withdrawing of the United Kingdom from the European Union, that was fueled by racist nativism and anti-immigrant rhetoric is foretelling of the fractures that continue to exist and the tacit rejection of the ongoing historical experiment of a "unified" and "globalized" world. Tensions continue to remain around democratic self-determination and human rights. The following chapter will first highlight the pitfalls of "prescriptive" peace education and further will address the very real tensions that exist when understanding and engaging in critical "peace" pedagogy and global citizenship and the challenges to incorporate them into official curriculum frameworks.

On Defining "Peace Activism"

"Peace activism" is an elusive term as the word peace in itself is utopian. How can we achieve peace on a grand scale as we are constantly bombarded with messages every day that the world is in great conflict, is oppressive and is deeply violent on both physical and spiritual levels? Peace, similar to diversity, has become a commodity. We "do diversity" here as we now "do peace work". "Human rights" have also become a form of currency as they are repeatedly utilized as a means to impose domination globally. These can be all viewed as feel good terms and can lend to a false sense of awareness and empowerment. Tackling with the concept of peace can help one to visualize openings, yet is limiting when only grappled with as static subject matter. Efforts to define peace sadly remain largely confined to the academic journals, institutional accolades and lip service to peace and social justice movements. Philosophizing in complex ways about theories related to peace and war make for very rigorous debate and can lead to self-affirmation and false notions that we are indeed deeply committed. Studies in the area of "peace" satisfy the theoretical and philosophical exercise to understand and deconstruct notions of it yet the interrogation remains within academic circles and scholarly dialogue. Mere theoretical readings in peace research can provide platforms for inquiry, however they lack the openings to advance political action. Schools and institutes of higher education are also guilty of using peace and social justice in their tolerance paradigms for recruitment and academic badges, yet at the very heart of these places systemic racism, sexism and oppression exist on all levels.

It can be easily noted that public schools have struggled to develop long-term engagement and dialogue about peace education. Conflict resolution and character building activities remain within a vacuum and rarely penetrate the larger school climate. Ian Harris and Mary Lee Morrison (2012) present us with some central modes of inquiry related to peace education, in particular

18 Seeking Peace Activists and Global Citizens

peace through justice and peace through politics or institution building. Harris and Morrison develop a thorough analysis of the challenges to peace education, its various forms and executions and further present simple guides on how to incorporate peace education on various levels. Their work essentially provides legitimacy to peace education as a deployable curriculum and further as an essential and workable component of the academic frameworks in educational institutions. These curricular frameworks, although essential for peace education to gain legitimacy as an area of inquiry, potentially reinforce certain perceptions. Namely, it emphasizes the perception that "peace" can be a product or outcome of carefully crafted peace education toolkits whereas I argue that "peace education" is potentially developed in relational ways and is a capricious process.

Betty Reardon (2013) offers us compelling arguments about the difficulties with peace education. Reardon states that, "little of the prepackaged peace knowledge we have has yet to prove adequate movements for political change. All that we know and all that we think we know about peace should be open to continual critical review and assessment as a standard practice of our pedagogy- at all levels and in all spheres of peace education" (p. 6). Reardon argues for all peace learning to be directed toward developing a range of reflective capacities relevant to political efficacy. Building upon these premises, Bekerman and Zembylas (2012) eloquently argue for the need to decenter and reframe the parameters of peace education and to analyze *critical pedagogies for troubled societies*. In their critique of peace education, Bekerman and Zembylas outline three core issues to consider, firstly, that perceived failures or dissatisfactions with the "products" of peace education has little to do with the quality of teachers and students and more to do with the quality of the systems that we cooperatively construct. Secondly, Western positivistic paradigmatic perspectives guide peace educational theory and practice and change can only happen when we have basic appreciation of the individual, of identity/culture and of the learning process. And lastly, educational solutions for peace education should be sought in the organization of present Western world politics rather than the limited parameters or school settings or the solitude of teachers and student's minds. Students and teachers alike should become critical design experts and begin to design a different path for reconciliation pedagogies (Bekerman and Zembylas 2012).

Understanding that schools and teachers reproduce hegemonic discourse and its overt and covert violence in schools, Bekerman and his colleagues pose questions about key debates around peace education and focus their work on "what makes critical pedagogies possible" instead of presenting a "toolkit" of practical pedagogical practices (p. 41). Pedagogies are also defined as relational encounters in place of classroom pedagogical practices. Bekerman and Zembylas's framework provides us with critical insight as we embark on our journey here to seek unofficial curriculums that in many ways could be framed as peace pedagogy being a set of relational encounters between teacher and learner. Bekerman and Zembylas also remind us that "peace education is not a thing (a reified knowledge that can be transmitted); second, peace education is a set of activities in the world and not a set of abstract ideas in the mind; and third, if we overlook the previous two points, we fall into the same epistemological mistakes of the West which has idealized, conceptualized (as fixed) and psychologized that which is human and its education. The main difficulty is that being trained as we (teachers, students, academics, policy makers, etc.) have been in the West, we find it very difficult to deal with a 'thing' without giving it a 'proper categorical' name; we seem to fear that if we do not speak about 'peace education' as such we will lose an area of specialization and thus go unrecognized or delegitimized in the academy" (p. 225). This argument is quite insightful and provides a key framework for the "unofficial" curriculums that I describe. The narratives in this book similarly cannot be categorized as a thing but rather pose real possibilities and opportunities for reflective and authentic dialogue. What do peace activists do? Is it merely sitting around a circle holding hands and singing "peace" songs? Does it mean putting yourself in the front lines of war to fight for a cause? It can mean those things or neither of them. Understanding "conflict" and violence is a first step towards peace. How is conflict understood and further, what is democratic about citizenship? Can we provide youth with opportunities to engage in counterhegemonic political action? Are there spaces where contested identities can explore authenticity? Where are the spaces where educators open windows of opportunity for students to be peace activists and global citizens? The two go hand in hand. Now not to be romantic about it, dialogues about peace, change and social justice, if they exist at all, tend to be confined to haphazard exchanges with limited influence. The opposing binaries of agency and complacency are so important to deconstruct and reminding students that one's participation in complacency is also a contribution to others' victimhood. Students also tend to be exposed to such issues in an all but tourist fashion.

Panayota Gounari (2013) reminds us that, "subjective violence always stands in need of spectators since it is through their gaze that it takes on meaning and importance, and it is the spectators' interpretations that make it what it is" (p. 71). Acting to resolve subjective violence, however, requires us to merely see a segment of a larger problem and oftentimes such activism simply aims to solve the symptom that is the root of larger systemic problems. Coupled with this, Gounari also argues that "there is a shift from the collective to the personal, from social issues to individual problems. Concerns for personal safety overwrite concerns of participation in the public sphere". Further going on to state, "Maybe that explains in part why often people so alienated in capitalist societies remain idle in the face of the violation of other people's safety, until their own safety is at stake" (p. 73). This is a powerful argument and serves to remind us about the difficult work we face. Panayota Gounari challenges peace educators to begin with defining what peace is not and to engage in critical engagement with history and thus allow students to take ownership of their own post-memory in order to begin raising questions about agency and subjectivity. In order to realize transformation, the intention and desire needs to exist amongst learners and educators. Without such intention or desire we miss variables in the equation and return to superficial tolerance paradigms that have little or no impact. To seek knowledge and burden oneself about the many forms of violence in the world, students and educators alike must be willing to engage and give relevance to these issues. An alternative socio-political and cultural consciousness should ideally be cultivated as students can be transformed from ordinary "spectators" to agents of political action.

Peace education scrutinizes the use of history in crafting identity and education systems that are often a "part of the problem" when inequality and inhumanity are present (Lange 2012). Peace education can illuminate the manner in which violence becomes normalized in society in structural (for example: discrimination) and cultural (for example: patriarchy) ways and teaches ways of being and seeing that struggle to be both culturally reflective and socially responsive and responsible (Harris and Morrison 2013). Because peace education is a form of transformational pedagogy (Boulding 1988), it is concerned with more than serving the current needs of a particular society. It is concerned with imparting principles and approaches that utilize nonviolence and champion reflective and responsive acts of learning (Bajaj 2008). According to Monisha Bajaj (2015):

> Whether schooling or sites of education themselves can achieve this herculean task of the elimination of all forms of violence at all levels is a constant tension in discussions of peace education and critical peace education. However, the belief in the promise and possibility of educational processes to contribute to social change efforts is largely shared among all peace educators. (p. 156)

Critical pedagogy and peace education can be woven together to develop, for example, pedagogies of resistance and to envision new structures to address violence and nonviolence (Bajaj 2015). Critical peace pedagogy is an essential starting point and is characterized by ongoing critical dialogue across disciplines, counter-positioning and disruption as well as participatory and engaged citizenship. Frameworks on such pedagogies of resistance as laid out by Jaramillo and Carreon (2014) that are centered in Latin American social movements can offer us a point of departure. Jaramillo and Carreon describe pedagogies of resistance as encompassing "reciprocity, solidarity and horizontalidad", or democratic and horizontal decision-making structures. According to an analysis by Bajaj, she argues that Jaramillo and Carreon's work can be taken to suggest that the contribution of "pedagogies of resistance" to critical peace educators is an emphasis on: (1) education that is meant to offer learners on the margins information that colonial and unequal socioeconomic processes have denied them; (2) methods of education that are accessible, engaging and democratic; and (3) educational processes that are linked to larger social movements advancing a vision of, and plan of action towards, greater equity and social justice (Bajaj 2015 p. 157). Returning to Bekerman and Zembylas's argument that critiques the "toolkit" analogy for peace education, these narratives in many instances illuminate the "relational encounters" that he purports and the ongoing dialogue or transformative engagement cannot be packaged as a "product", but rather are "experienced acts and enactments" for both teacher and learner alike.

In the current political landscape, social movements are gathering force from opposing directions and the tensions are real. We must be careful in what we assume and in how we frame our approach to disrupting mobilizations in the classroom. If students or educators adhere to distinct political positions that are oppressive, political action and interruption become increasingly challenging. We can take the example of Black Lives Matter and the Dream Act Dreamers who mobilize against violence, systemic racism and marginalization. At the same time, we have contradictory movements such as the mobilizations by Donald Trump's presidential campaign where hate and white supremacist groups mobilize around hate and policies of exclusion. Social movements mobilize around common belief systems. For example, we can take the angry white man movement, who is scapegoating immigrants for their positioning in society. These movements also use the status quo as their oppressive force and cry victimization from an "America" that has escaped them and has become "stolen" by immigrant populations. Blue Lives Matter was founded to support the legal defense of Darren Wilson, who was the police officer from Ferguson, Missouri who was placed on trial for killing the unarmed black teen Michael Brown in 2015. The Blue Lives Matter alliance is now focusing on law enforcement officers and has co-opted the message of Black Lives Matter. Critics argue that this agenda in many regards attempted to dilute and mock the Black Lives Matter message against prejudice. Blue Lives Matter has been linked to white supremacist ideology and has been able to receive widespread support and cloak its extremism behind the "badge" of law enforcement that commands society wide veneration.

Mobilizations around collective identities can be empowering or dangerous and understanding how these movements gain momentum is essential to analyze how they form part of larger hegemonic and counterhegemonic discourse. Engaging students in deep dialogue about complicated ideological forms can allow for a space of interaction to confound the tensions. Although tensions exist, undoing them is essential and at the same surmise critical peace pedagogy needs to intersect with a global citizenship education that is characterized by a politics of interruption.

22 Seeking Peace Activists and Global Citizens

Returning now to the aim of the book, why do these arguments matter for critical peace praxis? Monisha Bajaj (2015) argued for the development of *learner-actors* and for critical peace education to be an inquiry-based endeavor in order to have meaningful dialogue. The term *learner-actor* will be borrowed from Monisha Bajaj, henceforth in the book. One of the central questions explored in this book becomes then, keeping in mind that a distinct synergy need be in place in order to seek disruption and interruption-how can we foster meaningful spaces and counterhegemonic sites between *learner-actors* and scholar teacher activists to advance towards transformation and conscientization?

Global Citizenship and Interruptive Democracy

> I have defined interruptive democracy as 'the process by which people are enabled to intervene in practices which continue injustice'. It is an 'in-your-face' democracy—not just taking part, but the disposition to challenge. It is the democracy of the hand shooting up, the 'excuse-me' reflex. This means dissent, resilience and action, all within a framework of human rights. A democratic education has to handle identity and difference, it has to handle fear, and it has to take the risks of students learning from mistakes. We need to take risks too in doing unpopular comparative and international education studies.
>
> (Davies 2004 p. 212)

Globalization and the fluidity of national boundaries have served to empower racist nativism, first world-third world binaries and patriarchal forms. From the standpoint of lucrative business, globalization has set off a firestorm of economic gain for corporations and has allowed for the instant and digital interconnectedness of humanity. To define the concept of citizenship for an individual that situates oneself fluidly with deep commitments to transform both the local and global becomes complex. There are parallel threads that pertain to a young student's life in relation to global citizenship. On the one hand, it requires their careful and committed participation in realizing justice and upholding humanity. On the other, it requires that they be prepared to succeed in a global order in place of a small and localized geographic domain. Alongside the notion of a globalized, interconnected and fluid world, come the harmful effects of global neoliberalism, xenophobia and racist nativism. Carlos Mendoza (Torres et al. 2006 p. 33) claims a sense of urgency when outlining such harmful effects such as intense imbalances in concentrations of wealth, multiplications of urban masses that are unemployed or subsist with unstable unproductive employment, destruction and forced displacement of indigenous peasant populations, expansion of drug trafficking, disappearance of food security, increase in crime due to hunger, destabilization of national economies and maladjustment in local communities due to multinational corporations that ignore local residents.

In our day-to-day routine in communities and schools, is there a moment of pause to reconsider how we are all deeply embedded in these systems and participate in some extent? Does it appear to be an urgent matter to engage our classrooms in such topics? Torres et al. (2006) rightly state that unfortunately at this historical moment, the perceived social construction of globalization that dominates has little to do with respect for human dignity (p. 39). Torres urges a discussion to imagine or to believe in the need for a global citizen, or one who can rely on mutual loyalties and solidarities (p. 239). To imagine further, what might such multicultural democratic citizenship entail? For my students to first accept that they are very much embedded and participants in neo-liberal forms and agendas becomes crucial. The privilege of participating in the culture of power also requires responsibilities to change it. To further accept this and critically self-reflect on ways to resist these forms that they participate in and to seek social justice further turns this conversation on its head and can become the unofficial curriculums that speak to global citizenship and transformation.

Globalization is also multifaceted, and as Torres has previously argued, comprises four related forms including the popularly conceived neoliberal version, one ostensibly working to spread human rights and democracy, a third tied to terrorism and the war on terror and finally the loose confederation of organizations and individuals grouped under the label of "anti-globalization" (Torres et al. Introduction 2006). The third term, mondialisation, focuses on the solidarity of populations, building on universal human rights and international structures of governance while respecting cultural diversity (Torres 2006). Scholars have explored globalization through this lens, contemplating how democracy can transcend national boundaries by shifting beyond universal rights and freedom to implicitly explore questions of diversity and difference alongside the democratic principles of liberty and equality (Benhabib 2004, 2006; Butler and Mouffe 1997; Hardt and Negri 2004; Laclau and Mouffe 2001). Benhabib (2004) in particular argues for the need to explore and negotiate the conflicts of difference that she believes are a permanent feature in diverse societies to ensure that individual groups are free from political and communal limits on their freedom to associate and engage in politics.

Within the existing landscape of sovereign nation states, there are many fault lines where globalization does not lend humane and concerned global citizenship. In my previous work (2012), I have explored the question of "citizenship" and the deeply conflictual space that it can be for youth on the margins who struggle with belonging or not belonging. I explored what it meant for them to identify with nationhood and the global landscape when the messages around them told them that they clearly did not belong. Caught between Otherness and belonging, diasporic identities simultaneously adhere to multiple national spaces and can at various moments be neither here nor there. These identities are oftentimes adopted by choice. What becomes of those identities and "bodies" that are trafficked and enslaved and further taken across

24 Seeking Peace Activists and Global Citizens

borders? Is global citizenship an entitlement for those that can participate in forms of power and authority and are further legitimized as welcome members of global civil society? As world events and global politics ebb and flow bodies are rejected within national borders. Posturing against certain bodies within nations and rejecting their passage across borders plays into dangerous discourse that feeds into racist nativism. Given the unpredictability of world events, how then can one establish a sense of belonging and responsibility locally, nationally and globally? The universality of human rights or upholding the dignity of one another can serve as a point of departure. What have additionally been deemed essential are actions and dialogues that become forms of interruptive democracy (Davies 2005).

Nameless, faceless bodies are easily silenced as they are cloaked in anonymity and victimized by free passage across borders. In seeking justice for humanity, the universality of human rights has theoretically served as a point of departure. The force of law, however, is absent from UN declarations and conventions, hence, leaving human rights open to interpretation. Seyla Benhabib (2004) invites us to consider a future in which civil, social and some political rights be maximally unbundled from national belonging (p. 8). Benhabib eloquently elaborates on the example of the ban on Muslim headscarves in France to illustrate the tensions that can arise around efforts to realize homogeneity and national codes of belonging. Muslim women learned how to talk back to the state as their voice and self-understandings became reappropriated. She further argues that "these cases show that outsiders are not only at the borders of the polity but also within it. In fact, the very binarism between nationals and foreigners, citizens and migrants, is sociologically inadequate and the reality is much more fluid, as many citizens are of migrant origin, and many nationals themselves, are foreign born. There is incongruity between those that have formal democratic citizenship and others who are members of the population that do not formally belong. "The politics of peoplehood consists in their negotiation" (p. 68). She asks the powerful question: Will French traditions, for example, be less strong if they are carried forth and reappropriated by Algerian women or those of the Ivory Coast? The current burqini ban in Nice, France is also symbolic of the politics of nationhood being played out on women's bodies. Burqinis are viewed as violating French secularism and are being lauded as a fabric that symbolizes enslavement of women, yet beach-going nuns adorn full veils and skirts.

These debates have serious implications and reveal the nature of overt racist nativism. Reconfigurations of citizenship are taking place and nation states need be prepared for such shifts. As parameters are expanded and reconfigured in regard to citizenship within borders, what does it mean to engage in dialogue about seamless borders or global citizenship, especially when we continue to reconfigure and rewrite discourse of belonging within nations? As is being noted with the Brexit case, there was an immediate spike in incidents of racist attacks and targeting of individuals after the referendum. The "call to arms" to "return to a romantic mythical past" has bolstered right wing racism and the Brexit vote in many ways provides legitimacy and unspoken approval to target those that are claimed to taint and threaten English cultural values, norms and Judeo-Christian values. Let's take a look at the case of Islamophobia and terrorism and further the tensions that exist around "belonging" to nation-states.

In my first book, *Backlash: South Asian American Voices at the Margins* (2008), the terror attacks of 9/11 were the point of departure in my understanding of the victimization and revictimization of immigrant youth due to Islamophobic and racist forms. It was my charge to provide a personal voice and story to countless youth who had been targeted and profiled as "enemies of the state" due to the onslaught of media images, racist nativist sentiment and the war on terror. Countless organizations such as the Sikh Coalition and the American-Arab Anti-Discrimination League continue to send a counter narrative to oppressive discourse. The Islamophobic rhetoric is powerful and dangerous and has again become front and center in political campaigns. There is little critical interrogation about the messages that are being sent as it permeates our daily information feed. The sentiments of anger and misplaced aggression find victims in our everyday communities and further hate crimes are seldom prosecuted. We tread the same treacherous waters today. The terrorist attacks in Belgium, Istanbul, Nice, France and Baghdad symbolize an ongoing crisis. Messages both overt and covert are being disseminated in regard to an amalgamated identity of "who" the bodies are to hate and fear. It is immigrant, brown skin, beard, turban, Muslim, foreigner, accents, woman, hijab, Sikh, mosque, temple and all related markers that can fit this profile.

As I am reminded of a roadside billboard in Pennsylvania that I saw in December of 2015, *Jihadists Out-Christians In*, I understand how this can suggest that all of the above are marked as terrorists and are to be held liable. These billboards that incite anger and hatred are not to be taken whimsically. As the political campaigning of the likes of Donald Trump continue, everyday citizens may feel applauded and even justified in their hatred of others. The Trump Doctrine, strategically built upon Islamophobia, racism and violence allows such racist posturing and policing of bodies. The dangers of the current Trump Doctrine (as was previously the George Bush "war on terror") surface as rallying and mobilizing around hatred and anger becomes acceptable and viewed as a natural and almost patriotic response. Mobilizing around fear and hatred becomes a political strategy to garner votes. The sudden overt and covert acquiescence to utilize violence to "eliminate" and exclude the "Other" was being vocalized at Trump rallies and had been documented by journalists in the New York Times. In an article entitled *Unfiltered Voices From Trump Rallies*, journalists Ashley Parker, Nick Corasaniti and Erica Berenstein from August 4, 2016 documented the vitriolic language targeted at immigrants, the LGBT community and women. Trump and his followers have sanctioned the

26 Seeking Peace Activists and Global Citizens

unfiltered nature of this violence and hate and it is symbolic of the complicated hegemonic forms at work and its unprecedented nature.

The silence around his blatant statements was challenged to some degree, yet reinforced popular beliefs that are clearly oppressive. Trump had supporters that ranged from white nationalists, evangelicals and anti-immigrant activists. Unfortunately, he also rallied marginalized blue collar voters and found a scapegoat for their economic struggles: the immigrant body. Trump blamed immigrants and others for all things wrong in the world and this message resonated with folks who demanded an answer. His voice mobilized these groups with many others. He ran his campaign on a divide and conquer mantra and worked to create divisions and he had a very large platform where his message was being disseminated loud and clear. The Republican presidential nominee told a crowd in South Carolina he wants to block all Muslims from entering the United States "until our country's representatives can figure out what the hell is going on". He also said our nation would use its resources to round up every illegal immigrant and send them back across the border—no matter the cost. Trump's proposed ban, according to the Associated Press, would apply to immigrants and visitors alike, a sweeping prohibition affecting all adherents of a religion practiced by more than 1 billion people worldwide, as reported by the Associated Press. Trump and Brexit and most Rightist agendas alike adhere to mobilizations around nostalgia, a return to cultural memory, and a clear rejection of the concept of "globalized citizenship" and opening borders and parameters of defining the nation-state. Within these hotly contested debates, do we remain with but one lens, although a slippery slope, of human rights to engage in topics about the oppression of humanity?

Now let us return to the idea that global citizenship education should be interruptive democracy. Davies (2004) argued, "In terms of enabling schools to counter negative conflict, the idea of 'interruptive democracy', which develops the ideas of dialogue, encounter and challenge mentioned above in order to promote positive conflict in educational institutions". Davies frames global citizenship as a politics of interruption and disruption. From this interruption windows of opportunities arise for introspection and global citizenship requires an active critical participation. Davies argues for the need of a highly politicized discourse and engagement with multiple interrelated dimensions. It is a call to make the lives of others relevant and important-it is the call to uphold the dignity of others and their humanity and understand that universalism, ethnocentrism and cultural relativism can act as barriers to our understanding of diverse groups. Lynn Davies (2004) rightly states,

> Thus, a global citizenship education for peace would be a highly political education, not simply a bland multiculturalism, unquestioning 'tolerance' or 'being nice to each other.' It has four interrelated components: knowledge, analysis, skills, and action (KASA). First, there is the knowledge

of world current events, economics and international relations. Second is the capacity to critically analyze media, religious messages, dogma, superstition, hate literature, extremism, and fundamentalism. Third, it involves political skills, such as persuasion, negotiation, lobbying, campaigning, and demonstrating. Fourth are dispositions for joint action, which these days include networking through communications technology, starting a website, or joining international forums of young people working for peace. These are all essential ingredients for a solid global citizenship education for peace that can produce active world citizens who understand the causes and effects of conflict, who do not join radical groups, who vote out politicians who go to war, who do not support religious leaders who preach hate, and who join others to make their voice for peace more potent. (p. 4)

"Active global citizenship" according to Davies, requires the key components of student involvement in democracy and human rights in their schools. These conversations are rarely readily available or packaged in curriculum and it requires an educator who is deeply committed and willing to unearth controversial discussions and topics. Keeping in mind, nonetheless, that exposure to knowledge of others does not automatically ensure a level of acceptance, it is also not always to be assumed that those of diverse heritage desire their knowledge to be shared. A child, for example, who has fled his country of origin, may deeply reject his place of origin due to traumatization and feel compelled to block out or disengage from conversations. Given the landscape of policies and set curriculums there is no time in the day to incorporate these lessons or discussions, unless these narratives are part of an unofficial curriculum.

Human Rights and Dignity

By economy of human rights we mean the mechanisms through which human rights are developed, appropriated and circulated by state and non state actors, and then allocated unevenly to different individuals and social groups. Consequently, some groups may be bearers of a more extensive inventory of human rights and therefore be conserved more human than other groups.

(Introduction Perugini and Gordon 2015)

Along the journey to understand "peace" we are confronted with the idea of human rights and their universality. The United Nations Declaration on Human Rights has laid out thirty some articles on natural born rights, or points of dignity. Human rights, however, have become an area of social enterprise and have been largely left open to interpretation. Human rights have been argued to have become a form of "currency" and appropriated to impose domination. Perugini and Gordon (2015) in their book, *The Human Right to Dominate*, eloquently present the core challenges to the realization of universal human rights. With a focus on the Israeli-Palestinian conflict, they seek to uncover where in the name and appeal of human rights, violence and coercion has been legitimized and rationalized. Human rights are being used in dangerous ways to enforce domination and delegitimize others.

Under the guise of protecting "good" human rights, violently targeting "threats" to the interpretations of those rights are rightly justified. NGO's are also critiqued for their use of human rights as an organizing tool. Stating further, "The appropriation of human rights language, institutions and strategies by conservative actors points to an increasing convergence between liberals and conservatives on a global scale" (Perugini and Gordon p. 7). For example, pro-life and religious freedom agendas are increasingly affiliated with the Christian Right in the United States. There is a disorder around human rights being a part of a universalist project, they are not enforced, interpreted widely, and more specifically as a wide net concept and the human rights doctrine promises everything to everyone with little evidence to demonstrate the honoring of such rights. The imposing task then becomes for educators and their pupils to undo the packaging, marketing and appropriation of peace and human rights discourse. Taking on the task of a critical peace education, can students be encouraged to view the past and present with a lens that requires a deeply engaged and participatory framework rather than a distant, removed viewpoints as that if an onlooker? Can the eyewitness account be transformed into an activist and participant? Let me share a personal example of the challenges that can arise.

The Difficult Task of Shaping Peace Activists and Global Citizens

There are no answers and words of comfort in the face of senseless acts of violence as it cuts to the heart of humanity and the dignity of all people. We grapple with a range of emotions when we learn of such world events and the choice about how to act defines the moment. To begin with, it requires us to be very careful in our knee jerk response to world events. The caution is not due to a lack of empathy or humanity, rather it stems from the understanding that a balanced approach is needed in the inevitable urge to blame and annihilate all that we are taught to fear by media and hegemonic discourse. The "good cop, bad cop" binary draws on the need to create an immediate sense of closure and justice. Justice then is defined as an apocalyptic manhunt to catch evil and contain it. Contain it and destroy it, so we may go on living the good life. Never mind that in this global trek to defeat evil we have engaged in similar murderous acts, encouraged hatred in our communities and decimated entire communities' livelihoods. Fanning the flames of hatred is a choice.

After the Paris attacks in the autumn of 2015, I knew that we were just a moment away from the onslaught of hatred in the media and social media. Facebook profiles changing to the colors of the French flag signaled solidarity with victims. Measures to shut out refugees from Syria in Europe as well as the state of Michigan reinforced the complacency of labeling entire groups of people as terrorists and Beirut had been brutally attacked nights before in a similar terrorist act. There was silence about their tragedy and no Facebook profile of the Lebanese tree and no world monuments lit up in their nations colors. What are the lessons here as we engage in a hierarchy of victimhood? We clearly send a message about whose life is of more value as we pick and choose importance and these are the very discourses that are in need of interruption. Given this controversial landscape, how can students be encouraged to be activists in the face of daunting local and global social and political posturing that serves to divide and disempower communities?

If we are to interrupt these forms, it would require the work of educators at all levels to be careful not to reinforce or comply with rising anger and hatred. We must ask the more difficult questions, especially in the face of media messages about what "healing" should look like. Healing post 9/11 took on many forms, but largely a discourse of "being with us or against us" pervaded our airwaves. Of course, the majority of us would want to be with the "good guys" and with that comes an acceptance of who the "bad guys" are. The face of terror became the brown skinned bearded male and all profiles with these characteristics were to be feared, hated and eliminated. In my previous work, *Backlash: South Asian Immigrant Voices on the Margins*, I documented the struggles of a predominately Sikh community in the Midwestern United States after 9/11. Through the struggles to hide identities, forge assimilation and engage in overtly patriotic displays, Sikh youth understood on a very personal level the threat of violence to their identities and livelihood.

In the present moment, it remains just as critical to "undo" the discourse of hatred that is being incited by informal venues such as Facebook and Twitter. Digital citizenship as an avenue for dialogue is powerful for meaning making and mobilization. It comes, nonetheless, with responsibility. The ability to instantly connect globally with countless others can become a platform to interrupt or incite. The digital space has made it easier for hate groups to mobilize an audience and further not be held accountable for it. Prior to social media, hate groups relied on physical meetings, rallies and marches. In the current digital space, there has been an insurmountable increase in their presence and the ability to incite others with their messages.

For example, after the Paris terrorist attacks, social media was overwhelmed by gestures of solidarity with France. What does solidarity mean? Does it mean solidarity with all people non-Muslim? Does it enforce hierarchies of victimhood when we honor those killed in Paris and forget those in Beirut and countless others? Muslim communities have become all too familiar with the

30 Seeking Peace Activists and Global Citizens

scenario and in efforts to condemn hatred and honor their dignity and interrupting the larger framework of solidarity and its implicit Islamophobic stance is critical and is where the difficult work lies.

Holding a vigil for Paris at the 9/11 Memorial reinforces the parallels and validates the coupling of the attacks with Islamophobic sentiment. Facebook also had to apologize for not addressing the needs of other victims during Security Check features on it. These examples highlight the normalcy of anti-Muslim rhetoric and the manner it has become deeply embedded in societal response and that the initial messages have been sent about who matters and who does not. When children are empowered by this idea that they have a choice in how they react, it can lead to powerful lessons. I remind my students time and time again, that one has a choice not to hate, a choice to interrupt a racist comment, and ultimately a choice not to mobilize around hate. One can choose a different response, and sometimes one can choose to walk away.

The call to educators has never been so great as the world mobilizes again on the heels of terrorism. The challenges to interrupt these forms have also never been so challenging and difficult. A simple lesson plan on race or hate may not be enough, as students are immersed every day in messages about who belongs and who to fear. I said the following to my students the day after the attacks in Paris:

> Class, on Friday the world watched as an act of terror took place in Paris. These tragedies are heartless and frightening and have no justification Over the weekend, I had asked you to understand that this act could ignite hate in all forms and that given all that we had learned about global justice and human rights, I had asked that you disrupt or question misplaced blame and anger. I would like for the class to share with me if they had seen such rhetoric on social media.

The class raised their hands.

> Now I would like to ask if you want to share how you might have disrupted hate.

There was a pin drop silence in the class. Students shifted around in their seats and were reluctant to answer. I waited and waited. It was disheartening to understand the complacency, the lack of anger and the lack of activism. It was only after a very long pause that one student answered, "Well there was a lot of hate on my social media. I did not react. It was just raw emotion".

On my own campus, I believed it to be important to critically address moments of solidarity relegated for solely victims of Paris. A mixed message is sent that can easily reinforce rhetoric of who matters and who does not. Honoring certain victims over others only feeds into the larger discourse of oppression, hierarchies of humanness and racism. Such pedagogies are complicit with keeping enmity and anger alive.

An email to the campus Interfaith Center:

Dear respected colleagues:

As we process the tragedies of the current moment, I would like to ask that the Interfaith Center be sensitive to world events that have also victimized innocent civilians. I understand that today there is a moment of solidarity for "victims of the Paris" attacks. Can we also consider the victims of the Beirut terrorist attack? We are all victims to oppressive ideologies and I think it is important to have a more balanced approach in our recognition and honoring of victims—and be careful not to enforce hierarchies of victimhood.

Thank you for your kind consideration and support.

Regards
Dr. Verma

An email to my students in my classes

Dear Class:

As we take in the tragedies of the day, I can understand that you will be surrounded by raw emotions and reactions.

Given all that we have shared and discussed throughout the semester, I hope we restrain emotions of hatred. I am deeply disturbed by what I am reading around on social media. We have a choice in our response although this does not mean we validate an act of violence or tragedy—and you have become aware of so many acts of violence that happen every minute of every day.

I hope your families and loved ones are safe. As always, the work and voices of peace and human rights activists are the hardest ones to hear.

Regards,
Professor Verma

Students sat in silence and they felt deeply conflicted about what they saw around them and how to respond. They were silent as they understood that some of the knee-jerk responses on their social media feeds were related to raw emotion, yet we continued to discuss the value of interrupting these moments and the need to interrupt them as they had been armed with knowledge and an understanding to think critically.

I thought to myself that despite an entire semester of the discussion of human rights, I was met with silence when I asked students how they had disrupted

32 Seeking Peace Activists and Global Citizens

racist forms on social media on the heels of the Paris attacks. There was silence, and this moment illustrates well my previous argument that in order for transformation to take place, both learner and educator must have the intent and desire to be an agent of change. The term "agents of change" also demands constant deconstruction and understanding as well, since "change" can symbolize many things and the interpretation of what it means to work towards transformation is deeply political and can simultaneously be hegemonic and counterhegemonic. To borrow again from Perugini and Gordon (2015), "... human rights cannot be deployed in any other way, since every appropriation is a translation, and every translation is a form of politicization. Therefore the challenge is not to understand when human rights are politicized and when they are not. The challenge is to comprehend the ways in which they are politicized, and what the epistemic and political implications of these processes are" (p. 19). But again, this is not a reason to not begin, we begin and we hope and we begin again.

It was important for me to remind my students that apathy and silence can perhaps shape them to be passive consumers of misinformation that would essentially also make them complicit in relations of power. Legitimizing a violent counter attack to appease terrorism brings us back to the same dilemma of using domination to justify human rights. We begin to allot uneven rights and engage in a moral economy of violence as is argued in the book *The Human Right to Dominate* (Perugini and Gordon 2015). Requiring students to adopt a path of resistance and counter voice is a deeply personal process and as teachers and teacher educators it requires one to have patience and empathy. If it were so simple to shape activists, our jobs would have been done long ago. We must empower individuals to know that they have a choice in how they respond, they can choose interruption over oppression, they can choose to pause and disrupt racist forms, they can choose to not participate. In the classroom a teacher can engage in deeply political lessons to provoke thought processes and critical self-reflection and foster the agency that one hopes the individual carries forward. According to a study conducted in Sweden by James Leming (1992) on changed behavior and attitudes from a peace education program, less than 30 percent of participants indicated a changed attitude or desired behavior.

Leming (1992) goes on further to state:

> The changing of student attitudes and behavior associated with the goals of contemporary issues curricula appears to be a much more formidable task for school curricula than the teaching of knowledge regarding those same issues. Given that no clear relationship between increased knowledge and changes in attitudes and behavior was detected, the overall educational and social significance of the knowledge gains achieved must be questioned.
>
> (Leming 1992, p. 146)

There are many proposed ideas for what schooling for democracy might be or truly engaging multicultural education, for example the transformative paradigm of Sonia Nieto for multicultural education. Can these paradigms be analyzed in the framework of an unofficial curriculum? Perhaps this could also be understood as a site of compromise, yet a space where very real work and victories are made.

Unofficial Curriculum as a Politics of Interruption

As has been argued historically, schools are not isolated entities and are deeply embedded in local and global politics. Schools oftentimes become sites where nationhood, patriotism and nationalism are fostered. Distinct parameters can also be configured that send both overt and covert messages about belonging. This is where the role of teachers can begin, as it can become a lifelong process for the learner, the onus of responsibility is then passed to the learner to enact principles of disruption.

In the official curriculum, educators feel rushed, controlled and constrained to ever move beyond the boundaries set for them. A good school day is defined by "getting through" that lesson plan and getting the satisfactory test score. On a daily basis, we strip away valuable opportunities to realize the power of dialogue, the power of self-reflection and the power of transformation. With full understanding that the pressures on teachers serve to make them the scapegoats for all that is wrong with inequity and achievement gaps and with full empathy for the incredible burden teachers face to constantly "earn their keep", it is easy to forget the powerful agency that a teacher has in the lives of their students. Teachers have also been deskilled and deprofessionalized through the onslaught of teacher accountability and testing pressures. Teacher agency has become so far removed from the daily routine that to propose its importance and value is often met with sighs and resistance. Regardless, the classroom is where the dialogue must begin about peace and global citizenship. Peace activism and global citizenship cannot be "just another thing" to teach and it is essential that it be situated in the context of real lives. The difficult task becomes how to define these elusive terms and the abstractness can be disillusioning. It may not be that every educator will see its value and it truly is the efforts of those few teachers who take their calling to the level of activism and innovation. How can educators take the official curriculum and create pathways for reflection, peace, transformation and global citizenship?

Mandated, prescribed or core curriculum is taught on an average school day. These curriculums have set time frames, mandates and assessment tools. In the past decades, teachers have been drawn into larger policy frameworks where their curriculum is largely controlled locally and at times federally. The hidden curriculum has been defined as a space where dominant forms oppress individuals through definitions of official knowledge, legitimization of Eurocentric

34 Seeking Peace Activists and Global Citizens

histories and voices and delegitimization of the "Other" through silence and absence of diverse perspectives. Knowledge carried within students, for example, is also troubled and not neutral. What comes to be known as "official" or common sense become forms of power and are in need of interruption and interrogation. Hidden curriculum has been spoken about in relation to whose voice is silenced and how we normalize relations of power and legitimize official knowledge by what is overtly or covertly taught in schools. As is eloquently stated by Michael Apple (2004),

> Schools do not only control people; they also help control meaning. Since they preserve and distribute what is perceived to be 'legitimate knowledge'—the knowledge that 'we all must have,' schools confer cultural legitimacy on the knowledge of specific groups. But this is not all, for the ability of a group to make its knowledge into 'knowledge for all' is related to that group's power in the larger political and economic arena. Power and culture, then, need to be seen, not as static entities with no connection to each other, but as attributes of existing economic relations in a society. They are dialectically interwoven so that economic power and control is interconnected with cultural power and control. (p. 61)

I frame unofficial curriculum as the space between these two, the official curriculum and the outright resistance to it–the space where educators develop transformative lessons that are not in the daily lesson plan, they are "moments" in the classroom where teachers have rewritten or developed opportunities for their students that are creative and deeply critical and where they plant the seed to shape activists and global citizens. To occupy these spaces on the margins, educators are both engaged in the mandated curriculum yet need to be transformative and engage in critical peace pedagogy or with pedagogies of resistance and interruption. These counterhegemonic spaces are rich with dialogue and the unexpected and because of their unpredictability radical openings cannot always be realized. These unofficial curriculums deserve notice. An unofficial "marginal" curriculum can also teach students about how to answer back to those messages and be empowered. The unofficial curriculum that I write about is not on the official lesson plan but consists of narratives, conversations and unlikely lessons on empowerment and activism. It is difficult to accurately measure the enactments or mastery of subject of global citizenship and peace activism, hence there is the unlikelihood that they would ever become part of the official curriculum. Within an unofficial curriculum, students engage in understanding peace praxis as a relational encounter that is contextualized in the lives of others. Students learn to critically view the world around them and are challenged to view themselves as part of the greater society.

The space where *learner-actors* and teacher activists occupy is not always a definitive destination with a clear focus. We must remind ourselves that the victories are incremental changes that are difficult to quantify and therein lies the difficulty in packaging the process into a prescribed official curriculum. It is a deeply complicated space. These intermittent spaces and dialogues push the boundaries and limitations that are imposed by nation states and hegemonic discourse and allowing for rupture and possible reconciliation can mobilize those that occupy the space of the "Other" and disrupt those that "own" the gaze.

The "unofficial" space, on the margins of the curriculum, is where we will begin our conversation about critical peace activism and global citizenship. Having established a theoretical grounding for peace education practices in the current chapter, going forward it is imperative to analyze the challenges and victories that can arise as the bridge between theory and practices is navigated. The work of teacher activists to interrupt and engage in peace praxis is more difficult than ever. Teacher activists must navigate within highly restrictive curriculum frameworks with the added burden of high stakes testing and assessment requirements. There are examples of teacher activists creating radical spaces within seemingly impenetrable and regulated mandated curriculums. I would like to now begin the exploration within classrooms. Beginning inside a public elementary school followed by a chapter in a middle school, the voices of radical teachers who are critical peace educators will be elucidated and the powerful and meaningful dialogue that is developed beyond the core curriculum will take center stage.

2

THE COMMON CORE READING PROGRAM AND THE UNOFFICIAL LESSONS ON RACE

Readings on Roberto Clemente, MLK and Cesar Chavez

The "Let's Make Peace" curriculum box sat in the back of the classroom closet. Gathering dust, it had been partially opened. Broken crayon pieces and odds and ends pieces of construction paper were poking out of the box. An activity to color and draw peace doves was the opening lesson. The peace doves had been created the year before during a school day before the holiday break. "Peace doves" served as a good, creative activity and kept the students occupied. The doves were still hanging up around the classroom, their edges curled up with humidity of the summer. Carefully colored doves decorated the room and simple phrases were handwritten by students within the wings of the doves and read "peace is ice cream" and "peace is a day at the beach" or even "peace is a day off from school". I wondered about the impact of this activity on the lives of the students. Had opportunities been missed to engage in serious conversations about peace and conflict? It was a nice, fun classroom activity that provided the feel-good essence of doing "peace" education. Intuitively, art at the elementary age provides a productive outlet for students' expression. In this vein, the display was colorful and symbolic of "peace doves" or may have even signified the flight of students taking off for the summer. However, it again reinforced the toolkit and product dependent understanding about peace education; being a simple coloring activity with little sustained dialogue. Doing peace education with younger students can be developed in deeply meaningful ways and can be taken beyond the initial display of peace doves on the classroom wall.

Peace education in the elementary classroom is typically understood as an essential building block to character development, awareness and acceptance of self and others, conflict resolution and hopeful envisioning of a nobler world. As an ongoing persistent school philosophy, these hallmark efforts of peace education could serve a school community well. In many instances curriculum or dialogue related to peace education is fleeting and becomes a classroom "activity" for the day. Despite limited practice of sustained critical peace pedagogy, multicultural and critical curriculum theorists have historically advocated for transformative pedagogy in the face of measured gains and have continued to advocate for much needed change in curriculum. Mary Cowhey (2006) in her book *Black Ants and Buddhists* presents one of the most compelling arguments for the incorporation of critical engaging and "truthful" curriculum related to peace education.

Going a step further than the majority of teachers, Cowhey illuminates powerful classroom examples of elementary students exploring issues such as slavery, gay rights and homelessness which are topics that are merely skirted around or rarely touched upon in the younger years. Mary Cowhey states, "that as a teacher of critical thinkers, part of my job is to deliberately nurture sustained interest in questions over time". The stories in her classroom elucidate examples of students' ownership over their stories, provocative questions and problem posing investigations that they uniquely shape. The key word is "unique" here in that Cowhey's work became an unofficial spontaneous lesson that arose from students' interests and questions. This is again another example of how critical peace pedagogy takes on serious meaning when learners own their understanding and historical lens and further use authentic voices to inform further inquiry. Now I can imagine you might ask, given the current common core benchmarks, where is the time to allow for student creativity and explorations of peace and global citizenship? I beg to differ and will share real compelling examples of the realm of possibility.

In the current framework of common core, we might label certain developments as compromises. The emotionally charged reactions to the common core debate leave little room for discussion or agreement. Arguments range from common core being too challenging, it strips away creativity and common core as the death of public education. Critics claim that common core makes simple learning difficult. Further flaming the fears of opponents is the idea that we as a society have no hope or future ahead of us as we graduate students or "the victims" of a public school system that hails common core.

Some may argue that we have lost all our gains and are now at ground zero. I can agree to the fact that the heightened level of complexity in curriculum has required schools to take a closer look at their populations and provide remediation at an earlier age to ensure reading writing and math ability. High standards within the common core stoke fears about greater alienation for struggling learners.

There is room for debate however about how best practices, creative thinking and common core frameworks can facilitate complex and deeply profound lessons related to peace education. The purpose of this chapter will be to understand how rich common core multicultural texts are being used in the classroom to pose complicated questions in regard to peace, rights, racism and oppression. Children as young as 3rd and 4th grade historically have read limited texts and might not have faced the questions about race, segregation and oppression.

38 The Common Core Reading Program

Unofficial lessons that are being developed from common core readings can perhaps be understood as small victories and compromises and deserve some analysis and understanding. Can unofficial lessons in common core readings symbolize resistance and interruption? Are there lessons about global citizenship and peace building that can be developed from these common core readings?

The question also arises whether such compromises where teachers simultaneously enact core curriculum frameworks while engaging in counter hegemonic acts can be regarded as truly critical peace pedagogy. Such compromises, no doubt, represent the historically figurative double-edged sword as common core based curriculum represents an increase in curricular materials that reflect global and diverse contexts at the behest of profiteering for textbook companies and higher accountability for educators. These realities seem counterintuitive to critical pedagogy frameworks that demand a committed and serious engagement with knowledge consumption and the deconstruction of it. The current profiteering and control of knowledge and bodies in the classroom are neoliberal markets working at their best. I hold a deep respect for my colleagues that effortlessly defend their opposition to the compartmentalization of education and curriculum and further their deep distrust of the current trends in education. It will not be in the scope of this chapter to justify or reject common core benchmarks. Uncommon lessons and unofficial pedagogy beyond common core strike me and hint upon realms of possibility. Discussions about racial politics and oppression may be encouraged in close reading of texts and paragraph structure but we again must always ask the question whether such engagement with the curriculum can lead to lasting positive change. This moment of pause is clearly open to debate and it is imperative that we continue to ask the questions and inquire further.

There are, however, some dangerous arguments around staunch opponents of common core that are squarely situated in rightist and racist nativist agendas. In these instances, I fail to believe that there is any workable alliance between progressive critiques of common core and radical rightist groups. For example, in response to a 4th grade required reading of a story called "The Jacket", Young Conservatives outcry that:

> 4th graders are being taught that America is a racist nation and are being schooled to understand that they have "white privilege" based on common core readings. Young Conservatives claim that, "our children are being taught that, at its core, America is a racist nation". Conservative think tanks call common core an exercise in inhumanity as students are not reading "great works" of literature. Education Action Group (EAG) is lashing out with a strong assault on common core selections of readings. Outcries of indoctrination in regard to schools adopting the book *The Jacket* by Robert Clements in 4th grade classes shadow arguments that our schools are not teaching skills but rather are engaged in dialogue about white privilege and that is bad. The brief theme of the book, *The Jacket,*

is that the main character Phil sees a child wearing his brother's jacket and Phil assumes the jacket was stolen. It turns out he was wrong, and Phil has to ask himself the question: Would he have made the same assumption if the boy wearing the jacket hadn't been African American? This question leads the main character, Phil to some unsettling truths about himself, his neighborhood and his family. EAG also takes issue with *Harvesting Hope: The Story of Cesar Chavez* by Kathleen Krull that introduces 4th graders to the founder of the United Farm Workers union and lessons on equality. Teacher prompts are provided with this story to begin dialogue about inequality and unfairness as related to resources being heavily balanced towards one group versus the other, or an analysis of class based power. Young conservatives label this indoctrination of children and further turn them against America and its opportunity that it offers.

I am asking one to weigh the possibilities, albeit from a lens of discomfort yet moving forth with a word of caution. Oppressed voices, voices that were historically silenced, suddenly being incorporated into mainstream curriculum seem unexpected. Michael Apple may pose the question that one must critically analyze what the victories, as well as defeats are, for the subaltern. One must remain wary of such adoption in the curriculum. Questions are asked; our voices never mattered and now our identities are explored through part of a larger curriculum—why? We can now learn about issues of race and segregation in relation to the lives and histories of our great heroes, so where is the Catch 22? How can we tread lightly around this unusual alliance? Historically it would be counterhegemonic to read these stories and now they are part of hegemonic discourse. Is it that these stories have only been legitimized when neo-liberal markets have allowed them to be? Can it be that my voice and history now matter? For the sake of argument, this is indeed deeply disturbing and simply contributes to uneven relations of power. It speaks loudly about the control over curriculum, voices and bodies that gain validity only when "legitimized" by larger hegemonic discourse and political authority. These abrupt curriculum shifts in what suddenly becomes "normalized" in the classroom make the difficult and tireless decades of work by activists and multicultural theorists seem futile. The mere presence of diverse literature has little meaning without the very frameworks of critical engagement that have been put forth by multicultural theorists and these lessons are taking place unofficially separate from the official curriculum to bolster conversations about peace.

Progressive theorists have outlined key frameworks to fashion curriculum that is more inclusive, multicultural and anti-oppressive. Multicultural theorist, James Banks (1999) argues for the incorporation of five dimensions in order to foster multicultural education. The five dimensions are: knowledge construction, teaching different perspectives through literature, prejudice reduction, content integration and equity pedagogy. He also has proposed the Social Action Approach. This approach combines the transformation approach with

40 The Common Core Reading Program

activities to strive for social change. Students are not only instructed to understand and question social issues, but to also do something about important about it. For example, after participating in a unit about recent immigrants to North America, students may write letters to senators, Congress and newspaper editors to express their opinions about new policies (Banks 1999). Sonia Nieto's landmark work on the transformation versus tolerance paradigm also informs us well here. The transformation paradigm with its vital elements for school climate, teacher pedagogy, curriculum and student engagement remind us how complicated and arduous the journey is to realize it. Sonia Nieto (1999) reminds us that culture is dynamic and is influenced by political and social contexts, are dialectical and conflictual and inherent with tensions. Authenticity is highly contested. Albeit these movements present workable and valuable steps, there is serious work being done with common core readings with critical pedagogy to achieve the goal of active global citizenship.

Literary and grammar analysis are taxing work. Learning the mechanics of sentence writing and deciphering meanings in texts is an insurmountable task regardless of what the core readings may be. However, when grammar lessons are attached to rich literary texts, opportunities arise to take the lesson one step further. In New York State, common core readings for the 3rd grade were overwhelmingly populated by international folktales and short stories. Over 20 folktales were drawn from voices from Egypt, Myanmar, Burma, India and China to Native American stories. Women's rights and disability were issues that were also addressed. Ancient origins of our products, such as toothpaste originating in Egypt, are core readings. The core grammar lessons were related to text analysis and interpretation. Acceptance, transformation and critical social change cannot be packaged into a one step curricular lesson. Simply the presence of the literature has little meaning, sans the critical engagement with it.

As was previously argued, a mere "tourist" or "spectator" view of history and oppression remains just that, a spectacle to be had. Serious participatory work requires collective action, dedication and perseverance. How these works of literature are co-opted into the classroom can provide us with an opportunity to discuss and understand relations of power and oppression. The manner in which students are encouraged to shape an alternative view, or take ownership in memory and history can have a powerful impact. Through framing a meaningful historical lens, narratives and memories can be contested and reflected upon. At the elementary level, critical engagement with symbolic violence in history is tackled with as well as its lurking presence and educators are opening up the uncomfortable space to develop a lens to incorporate peace praxis in their pedagogy. Through creative thought, the core curriculum is being expanded and contextualized for rich discussions. In the scope of this chapter peace education, global citizenship and lessons about critical activism have been developed from 3rd and 4th grade common core texts. The unofficial lessons that were situated within real lives and contexts that were created by dedicated critical activist educators are essential to explore.

Common Core and Unofficial Lessons

The following classroom vignettes are drawn from urban and suburban elementary public schools in the New York area and are qualitative research based ethnographic case studies. The narratives presented were gathered through interviews and participant observation and fieldwork observation notes. Engage NY has outlined key readings that can be adopted in schools. Many of the lessons shared here are from school districts that have adopted these official texts in their classes. Teachers that are grounded in activist identities, in particular, engage their classrooms in unofficial spontaneous curriculums and are at the heart of this chapter. These educators utilize critical literacy to inform peace pedagogy. To consistently examine "why the world is the way it is?" is an opportunity to do more than understand language (literacy). It is an invitation to analyze how language is related to reality and therefore, that reality—as a constructed social product—can be different (Freire and Macedo 1987). Being critically literate, for critical literacy theorists, is acquiring knowledge of literacy that can be utilized and turned into action to further change the status quo. Such knowledge, according to Giroux and Giroux (2004), "is about more than understanding; it is also about the possibilities of self-determination, individual autonomy, and social agency" (p. 84). The creative pedagogic practices lend to goals of peace education. The objectives of peace education seek to illuminate how violence becomes normalized in society in cultural and structural ways and further teaches about the conditions of being and seeing that attempt to be both culturally reflective and socially responsive and responsible (Harris and Morrison 2012). The classroom examples that are shared illuminate such possibilities and the serious attempts that are made to evaluate the roots of cultural and social violence.

3rd Grade: Unofficial Lessons on Race

> Don't judge me, don't judge others, being good at something comes from inside of you and is not about your skin color.
>
> 3rd grade student

The classroom walls in Selena's 3rd grade class brought to life the diverse global readings with imagery and global mapping. Her classroom became a global landscape with flags and artifacts from the area of the world from where texts were being read in class. A folktale about the origins of toothpaste from Egypt was recreated with an area in the room dedicated to Egyptian artifacts, a space dedicated to quiet reading was in honor of Nasreen, the true story of Afghani girls who go to school secretly after the Taliban regime. Roberto Clemente Pride of the Pittsburgh Pirates story by Jonah Winter (2011), in particular, was the foundation of spontaneous lessons. The rich curriculum related to this common core framework defied boundaries and

42 The Common Core Reading Program

opened discussions for 3rd graders that were not previously conducted. The specific benchmark[1] for the 3rd grade English/Language Arts curriculum has been the platform for numerous critical discussions in 3rd grade classrooms. Roberto Clemente and the Pittsburgh Pirates reading selection tells the story of the life of Roberto Clemente and his struggles. The prescribed curriculum involves text analysis, vocabulary and grammar lessons. Selena, a peace educator and teacher activist, used the story as an opportunity to analyze issues of racial discrimination. Selena utilized a simulation role play in her 3rd grade classroom to allow students to understand how racism as a form of symbolic violence works in complex ways to minimize accomplishment and success. Coupled with written and discussion based self-reflection and further activist projects, students were able to put the story or Roberto Clemente in a tangible context for deeper meaning. When asked about her vision about peace education and the common core readings, Selena stated the following:

> Peace is much more than a happy one moment activity, I want to challenge my students worldview and then help them realize opportunities for peaceful or balanced judgement. I believe we are missing out on valuable opportunities to teach students about some very important lessons about race, judging others and fairness. I take time out of the schedule to engage the students in off the cuff discussions and I develop role plays to get the students to really think about what they are reading? Although it is not on the books, it is part of my 'personal' touch that I put on the material. To me this is peace education, it is not a hold hands in the classroom and sing "It's a Small World". Teaching peace is for them to understand that we are facing the same issues today as we did historically and we need to use the lens of history to understand the scope of the present and transform ourselves and the community around us.
>
> Selena—3rd grade teacher

During the school week Selena let the students know that they would be receiving stars on the board for good work and behavior and she was careful to not single out particular students and made efforts to provide a star to each student throughout the week. At the end of the week she looked around the room and gave out necklaces with medals on them that read "great work" or "superstar" or "class champion".

Selena, however decided that she would not award the necklace to students that wore the color blue that particular day. Five students did wear blue and were the students who did not receive a necklace. Selena allowed half the school day to pass in order to allow the students to commiserate and question why some had received credit and others not. The class was placed into small groups and was given a reflective assignment. Students were to write informally about

The Common Core Reading Program **43**

what they felt about the award system that was developed by Selena and if they would change it. Student responses by 3rd graders who received the necklaces for their efforts were as follows:

> I think it was a great week and we all received a great reward for our efforts.
> We all worked hard and earned our final success. I wonder why a few kids did not get awarded. Maybe they did not do their homework assignments.
> I feel great and I think we should have this every week!

The majority of the students were self-affirming and believed that they had earned their awards. It was only one particular student that took notice of the group that was excluded.

> I think it is not fair—we all had the same effort, why did a few students not get their final reward. Something does not seem right here. Maybe the teacher picked favorites?

This particular student removed herself from the group and went over to the group of student with the blue shirts. They chose to be in that group for the remainder of the class to express what they called, "showing support for my friends", or in other words, solidarity.

The five students who did not receive the necklaces were more pensive and critical of the activity.

> This is really unfair, we all did the same work—why is the teacher not recognizing us? I feel like the same effort did not get the same recognition.
> The teacher is making me upset. How come she forgot us?
> It seems like the teacher is picking on us.
> Did I do something wrong? I did everything right in fact I think I did more than the other kids who got the reward! I don't know why this happened.

Selena then took the moment to join the students in a powerful dialogue.

> Class, I want you to know that you all equally showed the same effort, so why do you think I did not reward these five children?

The students then answered with random remarks:

> Maybe they did not do homework.
> I know, they did not pay attention…

44 The Common Core Reading Program

Selena retorted:

> Class it was none of the above—I simply did not give them the credit because they were wearing the color blue.

The sighs and mood of the class instantly changed.
Students then responded:

> That is so unfair! Isn't that against the rules? How can you judge them because of the color of their shirts!

Selena then went on to draw parallels with the story of Roberto Clemente. Was he judged for his ethnic background, she asked.

> He was one of the greatest baseball players and was not given credit for his ability simply because he was Latino.

Racism, a form of symbolic violence, was a barrier to Clemente and few disrupted it. The disruption did not occur due to the reproduction of social attitudes and these social attitudes further led to more exclusion and violence, the very opposite of peace.

Selena had created a very important parallel world for the students in the room and the lesson was resonating strongly with the students. She concluded with providing all the students with necklaces and asked the class to do a reflective writing piece for their homework, asking them to write about how their experience was similar to Roberto Clemente and further if they could give him any advice, what would it be?

Student reflective pieces illustrated an opening of thought processes and critical self-reflection about racism, exclusion, judgment and fairness. The class discussion was also opened up about peace activism and advocacy. Students were reminded that when feeling powerless and misjudged, it can be difficult to advocate for what is right. As someone who might have a powerful voice, you can be an advocate and be a peace activist to undo stereotypes. The student who chose to move over to the excluded group was used as an example of an activist and advocate. The student shared her thoughts with the class:

> I did not feel right that the rest of the class sat away from the group with the blue shirts for no particular reason. I thought if I went and sat with them they would not feel so left out. Maybe this is what it means to stick up for others—when something is unfair.

Students wrote personal reflective pieces for their homework and had diverse understandings of the assignment.

> Sometimes we never give something a chance because we make a judgment about something. I have a funny story. I never liked to eat bananas. I just thought they looked funny and I did not like the way they would turn all brown and icky. In my head, I just said no and never gave them a chance. Until one day, we were on a long trip, I was starving and the only thing we had to eat were bananas. I refused for hours on the trip, and then finally, I agreed. It was the best fruit ever!!! I love bananas now. But my message is—sometimes we get so caught up in our minds that something is the way we think it is—like I thought bananas were horrible. When I finally gave it a chance, it was so great! I think we do this with everything in life—and it hurts people when we judge them for no reason—let's stop judging and give everyone a chance. Just like bananas, we don't know how many great things we are missing out on. Just like Roberto Clemente, he deserved to be celebrated for all of his talent no matter where he came from.

This very thoughtful reflection on likening judgment to their simple refusal to try a fruit is very telling. In the world of a 3rd grader this analogy and ability to reflect can begin a larger exercise on interrupting racist forms. This other example took a more serious tone.

> I feel sad when people stare at my father and talk to him like he is not smart. He wears a turban. This is part of his culture and who he is. We are Sikh. My father is a hardworking man and he loves to be in America. He can practice his religion and make a good life for my family. Someone in our family was beat up really badly. People were shouting to him—go away you terrorist. We are not terrorists—we just have different customs. My dad is like Roberto Clemente, a great man but judged for his culture.

When children take a lesson to a very personal level and speak of their personal trauma, teachers play a special role in facilitating and working through the tensions that may arise. The act of writing allowed students to reflect and validate their understandings about the life of Roberto Clemente and also took it to a personal level. Selena took the personal reflections and developed a collage for the class with symbolic imagery to represent the unique contributions of the students. Selena encouraged her students to become school advocates and develop opportunities to gain awareness and acceptance of the multiplicity of voices in the school.

46 The Common Core Reading Program

Following up on the lesson, Selena developed a consequent unofficial lesson related to the Roberto Clemente reading and required students to envision practical ideas to make a difference.

> Anytime you have an opportunity to make a difference in this world and you don't then you are wasting your time on earth.

Using this quote by Clemente as an example to follow, the classroom and their families developed the Roberto Clemente Make a Difference Project. The requirement that was sent home was to analyze this quote and what it meant for them and their local community. Students were then asked to create an idea for a project to make a difference in the local community or beyond. Ideas that were brought back to the classroom ranged from cleaning up the neighborhood litter and recycling to creating a Peace Park. The Peace Park would be a safe space to make new friends and to learn about the community members around them.

Directly related to racial politics, students presented the idea of highlighting accomplishments of all students in the school throughout the school year. This effort would allow all students to believe in their talents and be celebrated regardless of race or class background. The school administrators dedicated a wall at the school entrance to develop this grand display. Students were also nominated monthly for good character, attitude and citizenship. These efforts supported a larger school effort on anti-bullying that focuses and celebrates good character and efforts at being an upstander in the face of conflict. The upstander philosophy also supports the effort to celebrate one another. Students conducted a fundraiser to help support organizations like Roberto's Kids that support young athletes of minority background and seeks to bridge cultural difference with baseball. Students also spent a day cleaning up the Roberto Clemente State Park in the Bronx as a gesture of support. Selena has embraced the goal of incorporating unofficial lessons on the margins of her curriculum frameworks in her long-term vision.

> Peace education is not something you can take out of a box and do. It has meaning when it is developed spontaneously to expand the minds of your students. It is only when they are deeply interested that you can take them to another place ideologically. If you ask me what my next peace lesson will be, I couldn't tell you. It is not always something that is planned. But when it does occur it is meaningful and can be transformative.

MLK Turning the World Upside Down

The story of Martin Luther King, Jr. is generally a part of conversations in schools during the month of January during the MLK holiday and becomes a brief discussion during Black History Month. Peace education activities related to MLK Day tend to be a celebration of his life, a reading of the "I have a dream speech"

The Common Core Reading Program **47**

and perhaps a celebration of peaceful coexistence. This for the large part is simply the "heroes and holidays" curriculum. A required reading for 4th graders is *My Brother Martin: A Sister Remembers Growing up with Rev. Martin Luther King, Jr.* by Christine King Farris and provides an opportunity to engage in lengthy and ongoing discussions about race and segregation. Students were also required to read passages related to Nelson Mandela and Langston Hughes. Manuel, an area 4th grade teacher, designed an unofficial curriculum on race, oppression and segregation with the core texts. Manuel elaborated on his activism and desire to take the meanings of the texts to another level. His response greatly reflects his departure from allowing students to merely be "tourists" of great moments in history.

> I see in front of me these great works of literature that have profound lessons for the students. We are now expected to share readings with the students on great historical figures like MLK and Nelson Mandela. I cannot simply expect a grammar analysis from my students—I want them to dig deeper and understand how these moments of history are not history—that they are ever present in our lives, from our everyday interactions to the local community and finally out to the global arena.

To begin with, Manuel assigned the following take-home essay questions. Students were required to engage in a family reflection and write an informal response to one of the following essay prompts:

- What is an example of injustice that you have seen?
- In your own school, is there segregation in the lunch cafeteria?
- What is a dream you have for your future?
- How did MLK turn the world upside down?
- Recall a time when someone was treated unfairly. What did you do about it?
- Give an example of an act of kindness you did when no one was looking.

Students were given 1 week to respond to their essay questions. Manuel dedicated the afternoon timeframe at the end of the week to revisit the assignment and discuss what students had come up with. Manuel understood well that uncomfortable discussion may arise, yet he felt confident and obligated to facilitate the conversation. He began to discuss the responses that related to the immediate classroom and school environment in itself.

One student noted the following:

> Our lunchroom is separated out. Friends choose to sit with certain people and others oftentimes feel left out. The girls all sit together, and the boys too. Sometimes we notice the kids who are new to the school or are in ESL—they don't have any friends and are sitting alone. Sometimes I notice the kids that sit together are from the same heritage.

48 The Common Core Reading Program

Recess and separation was also elaborated upon by another student:

> Recess time can be hurtful. Sometimes the kids who can run faster separate out with the 'cool kids' and they play their cool kids games. The kids that are not as athletic feel left out. It is also not fair since the kids that feel left out don't really have a way to find someone to hang out with during recess.

Conversations began with analyzing segregation in the lunch room and this analysis spread further to understanding how our communities are deeply racially divided. Rarely touched upon as well, is the history of overt segregation and racist housing policies of the local community. Schools in these local area districts were entrenched in an ugly history or segregation and strict housing policies that rejected African American applicants. The students had conversation with their families about the historic underpinnings of segregation in their communities.

Student responses were as follows:

> Where we live we really needed a great leader like MLK—I am so surprised to know that we had laws against Black families moving to our neighborhood. That is so horrible and makes me even more happy that someone like MLK was very important to get us all to live together.
>
> My grandfather said something that bothers me, he was saying that it was ok that that 'those' families don't move here. I was telling him about what I was reading in school. I feel confused and I told him that maybe that is why MLK wanted to turn the world upside down.
>
> If we go back in time, I would not be allowed to live here in this neighborhood, it was written into the town code that Blacks can't live here. It makes me sad and maybe I feel a bit angry too. I don't want to think about it, it is a very bad thing that happened.

One student responded to the prompt that stated "If I visited MLK's childhood".

> Dear Martin, if I visited you during your childhood, maybe we would not be able to play together, live together or even go to school together. One day I would say I missed a chance to play with a great leader and know someone who was about to change the world. Maybe if you knew me maybe one day if I can make a difference—you might think you helped change my mind about how the world sees you and me.

Manuel's class touched upon local school based segregation in the lunch room to community wide histories of legalized segregation of housing policies MLK larger efforts to desegregate the nation and globally an understanding of the life and work of Nelson Mandela to answer the question? What does segregation look like globally? The work of Nelson Mandela has rarely breached the topics in the 4th grade classroom. As part of the larger parcel of common core texts, however, it provided an added global dimension to the conversation. Apartheid and Jim Crow laws were paralleled for the students as they came to understand the striking similarities. In response to an exit card activity in the classroom, what if MLK were alive today? One student poignantly stated the following:

> MLK would be happy and sad—he might feel proud that we have had our first African American president—but maybe if he listened to some of the angry things that people say, like Donald Trump, he would be afraid of the kind of hatred he has. MLK would have to fight again and say that we can't keep excluding people and being racist against people that look different from us.

This student response is a reminder that the work of teachers and students alike requires everyday vigilance and observation and life-long practices of being critical consumers of knowledge and dominant forms around us. Students in Manuel's class developed activist initiatives as well. Students developed pamphlets to distribute to all students about acceptance and inclusion. These pamphlets emphasized the vision of moving beyond tolerance and being proactive about subtle and overt behaviors that create barriers. Segregation in the lunchroom, recess and the bus were addressed. A multiple step guide was also created for teachers to adopt in order to foster inclusive activities in their classrooms. Finally, one student chose creative writing to express their understanding of the MLK readings and racism.

A Dormant Land—4th grade student
In a dormant land with nothing but sand, no birds fly above
In a horrible land, that's not so grand, there's no sign of love.
This is life with pain and strife,
No children and no life.
Fires blaze and waves crash on the shore
Not a single visitor at the door
No food in sight a world full of nothing but fright
While snow falls in the distance
All glares have malice
As the trees lie withered and black
The world is infected–pierced by the segregation tack
The chain of pain holds people in place
A gigantic sea of a pale white face
But we shall not let go of our beliefs of a blessed snow
To end all of the racism as we know
We should never forget the lessons of life
Let us tackle the strife
Up above, the great clouds
Help us escape as the darkness shrouds.

50 The Common Core Reading Program

As students and teachers come to understand how race and oppression touch their everyday lives, the legacy of these unofficial lessons remains to be revealed. I believe Selena and Manuel embody the characteristics of "activist" identities. They have taken the prescribed curriculum and developed meaningful lessons, we may call them-anti-oppressive, controversial, critical, but ultimately they are grounded in their abilities and desire to "take back" and "speak back" to dominant forms. Within the context of the students' lives, histories and identities, the teachers have pushed open conversations about institutionalized racism and made possible the grappling with ideas about "peace".

At the elementary level, students are invited to contend with systemic violence and consequently to think critically about contemporary realities with their own unique "post" memory lens. Their teachers have decentered the structures of their thinking and have encouraged critical ways of knowing. Armed with a critical lens about institutionalized racism they can become peace activists through deliberately being mindful of exclusionary practices and racism. The sustained nature of the student's inquiry is critical. Manuel's students continued their dialogue about issues of segregation and racism throughout the school year. Students were encouraged to develop school wide initiatives to combat self-segregation and exclusion. Oftentimes, these conversations were opened up at their dinner tables at home, and reflections continued to be shared about the topic. At the end of the school year, students had the opportunity to meet a guest speaker who spoke about apartheid in South Africa. This guest speaker provided the students with stories of their upbringing in the apartheid state and their experiences with racism. Students decided to keep a long-term connection with the speaker through ongoing letter writing and documentation of their sustained vision of creating a more peaceful and inclusive school climate. None of these experiences and activities was officially documented in the curriculum, it was within the unofficial lessons that students were exposed to the most profound curriculum. In conclusion, I would like to share a third example of activist teaching based on readings on Cesar Chavez.

Building Fences and Walls: Being Cesar Chavez

A powerful example of a classroom where current day politics is brought into the classroom through opportunities found in the readings can be illustrated by Saira's 4th grade classroom. Imagination played an important role in Saira's class and was central to building peace awareness in her classroom. Saira utilized dramatic and serious play to invoke meaningful lessons about peace with her students. In support of documented research about play, Arlow (2004) states the following "playfulness and even a degree of naivete are integral parts of imagining ... but imagining is not the end of the process ... students are encouraged to find practical and realistic ways in which they can narrow the gap between the world as it is and their future community, by developing the skills necessary to engage in democratic processes. In doing so they are exposed to alternatives to violence (Arlow 2004 p. 285). The assigned class reading was the 4th grade common core reading on *Harvesting Hope The Story of Cesar Chavez* by Kathleen Krull. This powerful reading provides young students with an opportunity to grapple with issues of human rights, workers rights and the plight of migrant workers. Themes that arise in the story are for example, worker rights, enslavement, racism, white trade only and the National Farmworkers Association and the victory for farmworkers.

Saira, a teacher activist, used *Harvesting Hope* as a platform to discuss many valuable lessons with the class and her unofficial lesson on building walls illustrates the connections she made with in class readings and the contemporary political climate. To begin her lesson, Saira used some key questions related to the story to promote in class discussions. In Cesar's words, "It is well to remember there must be courage but also that in victory there must be humility". He urged people to take action with words, not violence. Saira posed the following questions to her students: What were the things that Cesar hoped for that made him find a way to talk people into joining his fight for justice? How did hope help Cesar to overcome his shyness and become a leader? How do Cesar Chavez and other activists like him instill hope in Latinos, farmworkers and other people?

Students then responded with the following:

> Cesar Chavez like MLK fought for an important cause. It is not right that people have to work long hours and get hurt by the work they do.
>
> It is very sad to read about his life and the hard things that he faced. I don't know if we could ever imagine working long hours in a farm and sleeping on a dirt floor.
>
> He fought for his people with peace and did not use violence. That is a good lesson.
>
> Chavez represents hope because he never gave up and everyone followed him when they had a march. He was able to use his peaceful ways to become a great leader.
>
> When we have student council in school we are also using peace and group leadership to make changes at school, Chavez did all that on a very big level and he won.

Saira wanted to take the lesson one step further to analyze the idea of building walls and fighting for rights. Saira said the following to the class:

> Class, the story of Cesar Chavez's life is very inspiring and it provides a good example about the life of migrant workers and the way they have had to fight for their rights and their voice. The unfortunate part is today we continue to have many migrant workers who work on farms that are

52 The Common Core Reading Program

still not protected and face similar hardships that Chavez faced. There are, however some ideas that are being explored on how to understand the needs of migrant farmworkers who are very vulnerable since their human rights are not upheld. Tomorrow in class we will discuss these ideas.

The following day, Saira put up a physical wall that divided the classroom. One the one side she randomly placed half the class, and the other half behind the wall. The wall was made of cardboard and was high enough that students could not see one another. As students walked into class, Saira directed them to either sit behind the wall or in the regular classroom. She told the students the following:

> From today onwards, a gigantic wall has been built to stop all individuals from coming into the country. This wall represents a statement from a country that it is shutting out all individuals that come here to work on our farms as migrants and who do not officially belong. You can no longer come over to the land called Saira Land. Because migrants play a big role in our economy, we will no longer have fruits and vegetables in our lunchboxes and many other items will be missing from our daily lessons because we will have lost a large part of our labor force. Students were asked to then research walls and fences designed to separate communities—they were asked to bring research to class the following day. Students were also asked to use crayons and markers to write their feelings and thoughts on the physical wall.

Statements that students put up on the wall were as follows:

> Walls hurt, please let us in.
> Words can bring down barriers—walls try to shut people out but we will continue to speak our minds.
> Let's bring down the walls and honor the history of Chavez and MLK who came before us.
> Is this what Donald Trump wants? This is not the answer.
> Telling us we are not allowed will stop our bodies but not our spirits and hearts.
> Our neighborhood used to not allow black families to live here, once upon a time we could not go to school together—we want to be together.
> Human beings are not to be trapped and shut out—human beings should come together.

Students artistically created images of peaceful landscapes and had also drawn world flags in harmony. Students returned to class with many global examples of fences and walls that have been utilized to separate nations. Information was

The Common Core Reading Program **53**

shared about the Berlin Wall, the Great Wall of China and the walls that were put up during the Syrian crisis in Hungary, as well as the fences that went up along the Southwest border after 9/11 as well as the Israel-Gaza barrier. Students presented insightful analysis about the larger negative message that can be sent about these physical walls. Referring to Cesar Chavez, students also reminded one another that his story was about a non-violent effort to secure workers' rights and human rights. Students stated that workers that come today must also desire the same rights and their migrant pathways are largely based on livelihood and survival. The class also continued to make the connection with policy ideas of building a wall to close off Mexico to the United States. To sum up, I will share one student's essay on the Building Walls activity.

> We always have tried to build walls to separate people or shut people out. We can now see that peace was never achieved from walls. Peace can come when people like Chavez fight for rights and peacefully seek to be treated fairly. Imagine if every country in the world had a big wall that would not let us move between borders. We would all be like bubble people—stay in our own little bubbles and never see each other. The world would be a bunch of bubbles and it would make the world a very sad place.

In a gesture of solidarity, the class brought down the physical wall in the classroom together and then displayed the wall in the school hallways. Student comments and art that had been added to the wall during the activity was visible for all to see, and most importantly the painful process of separation, then reunification served as an important reminder to the school community about the importance of being critical and participatory global citizens. As was previously shared in this chapter, the story of Cesar Chavez provoked a reaction by rightist movements as it was deemed un-American and inappropriate for the 4th grade classroom. Saira's efforts to not only engage her class with the reading, but to further create an unofficial lesson with it, makes her work counter hegemonic pedagogy of resistance in multiple ways.

Activist Identities

The educators highlighted in this chapter in every way share the profile of "activist identities" that Michael Apple has described in his book Can Education Change Society? (2013)

> Actions that are in social movements close to home change people. Such actions give people activist identities and teach strategies that echo throughout society, ones that can be and are taken up in other struggles. (p. 153)

These teachers are transformative individuals and enact pedagogies of resistance and critical peace education. Their work beyond the prescribed curriculum illustrates the counter space that I previously described. Activist identities clearly view their role as transformative and their ability to work the in-between spaces of the requirements of common core curriculum to have intense conversations and profound debate on issues or race, exploitation and discrimination is creative and powerful. They engage in interruptive democracy and call to question and disrupt forms, and further encourage their students to imagine possibilities for change. These teachers did not surrender their critical work under the limitations of common core benchmarks. They are creating linkages with the past and the present and demanding that their students use their historical lens to interpret the present day. Students are provided with the charge to become what Zvi Bekerman and Michalinos Zembylas (2012) have described; "critical design experts". As "critical design experts", students and educator alike "recognize and critique how the world is designed and how it can be redesigned" (Bekerman and Zembylas 2012). As peace activists, these educators are "prying the lever" open and facilitating the awareness of uncomfortable truths and violent historical memories that further give serious meaning to the works that they read. Leaving these activist classrooms with greater awareness of the world, students have become aware of their own agency to participate democratically. Schools have the potential to serve as radical sites of change and through these powerful lessons in the classroom and learner activists can begin to branch out to the larger school climate and ultimately engage in social movements. I would like to end this chapter with one more powerful poem written by a 4th grade student about slavery.

<u>The Maiden</u>
The maiden strolls across the woods
Carrying the swarthy men's valuables and goods
Taking every man's command
Yet she feels out of place in the land
She hears the howling breeze
And sees the beautiful blossomed trees
While touching the blossoming leaves
She skips rocks across the clear lake
Loving every creature, even the snake
She bakes everything from cake to bread
The appreciation of her is as stale as lead
She lives her life—put in chains
The only water she gets is when it rains
With one mistake comes spiraling rage

She goes to the woods to escape the cage
Awakening under a large oak
Her entire village was starved and broke
The maiden lives now in prosperity and peace
She is no longer put under a leash.

This chapter has provided a compelling case for creating openings for peace education practice in the elementary classroom. A recurrent theme in these classrooms has been the relation between segregation, racism and violence. Conversations about walls and segregation prompted the greater need to analyze school and classroom climate further, possibilities for peace were explored in student work as well as in student led collective activist projects. These projects focused upon the role of social climate and belonging in the school and community culture. Now moving on to the following chapter, I would like to visit Mr. D's middle school classroom. Similar to the activist work of the elementary school teachers, Mr. D finds unofficial spaces within his classroom day to allow his students to seriously reflect on violence and possibilities of peace through the medium of imagery and photographs.

Note

1 CCSS.ELA-LITERACY.RL.3.2

Recount stories, including fables, folktales, and myths from diverse cultures; determine the central message, lesson, or moral and explain how it is conveyed through key details in the text.

3

MY STORY OUR STORY

Interpretations of Global Violence and Peace in the Middle School Classroom

Twice a week when the clock strikes 2:00 p.m., there is a remaining half hour to the school day. It is at this time that Mr. D's Social Studies classroom ends the official curriculum of the day. This final half hour becomes a critical and radical space in the school day where teacher and students alike mutually explore and interpret possibilities for peace in the face of acts of violence. This chapter will document narratives from a middle school classroom where Mr. D, a teacher activist, engages his classroom in ongoing dialogue about the cyclical nature of violence through imagery, empathy and photography. Tying together the past and present allows students to "walk in the footsteps" of historical moments and further develop their own critical post memory lens. From this lens students analyze collective stories from a letter exchange project with refugees and recast meanings about peace: it's where my story is shared as our story.

Imagery can be powerful and allows students to develop critical and thoughtful interpretations of its meaning. Within textbooks, however, images are presented with captions and guided questions that prompt the student towards a predefined answer. Mr. D experienced frustration when implementing various lessons in his classroom from the curriculum agenda. In particular he believed students were being limited in their voice and their ownership of their understandings of historical images. As a pedagogical tool, experts in the field argue for the inculcation of historical photograph analysis to the forefront of social studies education (Barton 2001; Coventry et al. 2006; Madison 2004; Waters and Russell 2012; Werner 2002) Students gain critical insight with glimpses into past cultures, and hence reveals to students eras that have long since disappeared (Levine 2004). As some researchers indicate, the moment students use their hearts as well as their heads to interact with the past, those feelings transfer into lasting memories (Berry, Schmied and Schrock 2008; Zull 2004).

Several studies have concluded that memories, experiences and interactions with visuals arouse emotional reactions that can lead to lasting cognitive effects than those that do not (Goolkasian 2000; Hamann, Ely, Grafton and Kilts 1999; Kensinger and Corkin 2003; Levine and Pizarro 2004). In addition to cognitive impact, a close consideration and analysis of photographs may also heighten students' cultural awareness and empathy toward others (Woyshner 2006). Although there is strong support in the research to hone visual and media literacy skills in students, it tends to be commodified into a packaged lesson plan with overly focused parameters. As Felten (2008) notes, "living in an image-rich world … does not mean students … naturally possess sophisticated visual literacy skills" (p. 60). Coupled with frustration with the curriculum and the obvious apathy his students exhibited in regard to national and global events, Mr. D crafted spaces to expose his students to more meaningful and critical discourse. Mr. D shared the following reflection about his pedagogy:

> As a social studies teacher and a peace activist, I believe there should be a continual dialogue in my classroom about violence in the world and alternatives solutions to violence. Prepackaged social studies content is devoid of open-ended discussion. Historical events are so incredibly disconnected to students' lives. They fail to see the connections between history and the present. Students roll their eyes, are bored, and are clearly not interested in these scripted lesson plans. For me, it is an imperative part of my role as an educator to provide my students with the opportunity to get personally involved and connected with the past in order to understand the present. We live in an era when history is being replayed before us daily. There are so many key connections that students need to make. Violence in every form is all around us—do they understand the roots of this violence? Are they opening up the newspaper to update themselves on the state of the world? Do they understand terrorism? Brexit? Trump? Do they believe violence is the means to achieve peace? I want them to transfer these skills to the outside everyday world. If my students learn to make the connections and develop empathy in the face of hate, seek peace as an alternative to violence and can be empowered to disrupt oppressive forms, I may have been a good teacher after all.

Mr. D allowed me to be a participant observer in his classroom and in the following chapter I will share highlighted student work that connects contemporary global events to the past in deeply meaningful ways. Through visual literacy, students are presented with a historic image and provided the title and year when it was created. The task then becomes for students to reflect and transplant the experience in the image to the present day. Students bring

58 My Story Our Story

in contemporary images that share a similar trauma or tragedy and write a creative narrative from first person voice related to that image. Current day global events and violence are then connected to the past and students are asked to interpret and analyze the similarities and envision possibilities for peace. By learning to read images and media as "texts" students can discover ways they directly connect to movements for social justice (Segall 1999) and learn about themselves and others (Segall, Heilman and Cherryholmes 2006). These examples further add insight about the process and development of spontaneous and critical peace education and activist projects in the unofficial classroom space.

I Am a Man

In 1968, Ernest Withers photographed a powerful scene of African American sanitation workers on strike in Memphis, Tennessee. The workers on strike held placards that read "I am a Man". This slogan was used to protest and strike down legalized segregation, dehumanization and the evils of humanity during the Civil Rights era. This image was shared in the classroom and students were asked the following by Mr. D:

> Right here in front of you is a powerful image taken in 1968. The title of the photograph is "I am a Man". This image speaks about segregation, violence, racism and racial profiling. I would like for you to look carefully at the image and imagine what is taking place, what are the emotions— but most importantly what do you believe the forms of violence are? Your task will be to transplant the reflections you have from this image and bring to class a contemporary image that sustains the same message and ideas about violence and dehumanization. You are to write a short reflection related to your selected image and speak about what you are experiencing. You will be the voice for the image.

Students were provided a challenging task, yet the students felt emboldened to connect the image to the present and give it personal relevance. As an open-ended task, students were given a space to be creative and critical. Two students in particular challenged the class to explore facets of everyday racism that they encountered in their own lives. Student A brought in an image from the Ferguson riots of a man donning a spin off the protest slogan of "I am a Man" to "I am Michael Brown". Student A wrote the following narrative related to their image:

> I am Black and I am a Man. I am Michael Brown. There is no justice for my death, but please remember that I am a human being—I am blood, flesh and bone and share that with all humankind.

Student B brought in an image of a protester being stared down by armed police officers. This image has also been captured historically during the civil rights era.

> Yes, I am standing here staring right at the end of your rifles. I am a woman who demands an answer. Am I not allowed to move beyond this line because of the color of my skin? Why do you control me with threat of violence? Can we shake hands and make peace? Or will I be arrested if I extend my hand out to you? Do I dare?

Mr. D asked the class to reflect on the student narratives and he placed the contemporary images next to the 1968 photo of "I Am a Man". The most important moment was to analyze that despite being decades apart that the three images were eerily signaling cycles of social unrest and violence that have yet to be interrupted. Student C opened up the difficult dialogue with the following comment:

> We have stood still in time because we have never learned not to hate.

This confession and assertion crafted a raw opening in the room. The honesty was noble and held all individuals in the room accountable to self-reflect. Mr. D understood the weight of the moment and created an opportunity to envision possibilities for reconciliation. The sense of urgency to address these issues was real and he understood that very few educators were willing to venture into this conversation with their students.

Through using the student written narrative by Student A and Student B he asked the class to respond to the imaginary commentary. The responses would be confidential and deposited in a box outside the classroom during the school week. This technique allowed students to feel safe in their engagement with such controversial issues as well as a chance to be honest without fear of being on display in the classroom. With respect to student privacy, Mr. D did not share student responses openly with the class, he did summarize for the class that hate and racism continue to permeate our everyday lives and that incredible strides have yet to be made to combat the violence we see in our communities. In the wake of racial profiling and the killing of young African American youth as well as the recent ambushes and killings of police officers, the students in Mr. D's class faced many difficult questions.

Mr. D encourages active engagement with these issues and uses everyday acts of violence as a platform for discussion. I frequently observed him engage his classroom with thought provoking inquiry. Mr. D would ask his class, "What are the questions we should be asking related to this issue?" Beginning with such inquiry the students believed it was safe to question, interrogate and even disrupt symbolic forms of violence. The debate between the goals of

60 My Story Our Story

Black Lives Matter and Blue Lives Matter took center stage in Mr. D's classroom space as well. This was a difficult dialogue to navigate because students felt so strongly about their viewpoints. Students were quick to understand that creating an opposing scenario between Black Lives and Blue Lives was feeding the fire of hatred and separation. Co-opting the Black Lives Matter campaign against prejudice with other counternarratives was viewed as damaging to their message. Students also were keen to note that ongoing opposing binary nature of these parallel movements only serve to divide communities further. As Mr. D reminded the students, what are the questions we should be asking and why has society failed to interrupt these violent forms?

The class further tackled this question with a collage in the classroom entitled "Alternative Solutions to Violence". In particular, when analyzing racial profiling and police brutality, students believed it was important to create partnerships between communities and law enforcement to foster mutual respect and concern. Students focused on the issue of dignity and justice for all members of a community and were forthright in their empathy with communities that have long been entrenched in racial prejudice and exclusion. Mr. D understands that the topic of Black Lives Matter may never make its way to a formal textbook. Textbooks work in 7 year cycles and the vetting process for new materials is complicated. The knowledge that is absent in many ways sends the message to our students about what does and what does not matter. It is when teachers like Mr. D understand the importance of matters of social and cultural violence and develop unofficial curriculums that are deeply reflective, radical and political that important dialogue can take place.

My Story Our Story: Home

In 1948 in Poland, David Seymour photographed a young girl who was born in a Nazi camp. The photograph portrays the young girl drawing her home The title of the image is "Tereska Draws her Home". In the image, a young girl stares out at the camera and on the chalkboard behind her she depicts her home as a series of spiraling chalk circles. Quite obvious to the viewer, the concept of home is absent from this young child's life as her childhood, livelihood and humanity have been stripped away from her. In relation to the Syrian refugee crisis and the anti-immigrant rhetoric towards undocumented Mexican families, Mr. D hoped to draw the correlation with Tereska and current day events.

> I would like for you to look at this image called Home. Reflect upon what emotions you can sense from this young girl and her depiction of home. Home in the image is chaotic, abstract, and is depicted with multiple lines and circles coming together. Your task for this week will be to transplant 'her struggle to identify a home' with current day populations

that are displaced, stateless and homeless. Finally how might home be located and provided? Bring in imagery that depicts these sentiments today. And remember to write a creative narrative about the image.

During the timeframe that Mr. D had presented his class with this imagery, multiple global events were acutely relevant to this class dialogue. To name a few, students could also focus on the kidnappings of young girls by Boko Haram in Nigeria, the rejection of undocumented immigrants in the United States and various other examples of homeless individuals who struggle to realize a safe and secure place to live and call home. Student responses to the assignment were thoughtful, critical and quite radical. The encouragement to take ownership of their historical lens to analyze the past and the present was provoking authentic connections for the students. The classroom became a transformative site to question and develop alternative imaginaries.

Student C brought in the image of the deceased toddler on the beach shore in Turkey named Aylan Kurdi.

> I have left this world now, I am a small baby—my parents took me away from my land to find safety—food, shelter, education, a new life—a new home. My life ended very young–I will never know the world for all its beauty—please make room and love for other children like me–we ask only for a safe world to live and grow up in.

Student D chose to write a narrative about young girls who were kidnapped by Boko Haram.

> I slept in my mothers arms one night and awoke to strangers beating down our door—it was Boko Haram. I was kidnapped-stolen-taken away—I have not ever been back home—my home is now a world of darkness, violence and trauma. I am not who I was when I was taken that night—now I am what Boko Haram wants me to be. Home is the jungle, home is fear, home has been stolen.

Finally, Student E shared an image of a wall in order to speak about the divisions these borders will create.

> My land was sliced like a pie. It was given a name. I was told I no longer belonged. The pie was all taken away, leaving me with dust and an empty bag to carry back to nowhere. There is no longer a home. Home is occupied by a name. A name that tells me that I am not wanted. The home I want is not home. The place I was told is my home does not feel right to me. Home will be my empty bag and where my footprints can lead me. Perhaps near or far—but home will not be there.

The level of thought and meaning in student reflective work was moving. It became obvious that students were compelled to take ownership of their interpretive lens and then take their analysis one step further. Through demanding empathy and dignity for the silenced and forgotten victims that they speak for is transformative. A resounding thought amongst the students, related to this particular dialogue, was the compulsion to develop an activist project to make a meaningful impact on the lives of displaced individuals. What this project would be was the topic of serious debate for several months. Students wanted to have full ownership over the project, long term sustainability and demanded that it be low cost. Hence, a letter writing partnership with refugee children came to be and was called "My Story Our Story: Letters for Peace". Through partnership with a local refugee organization with basecamps in regions throughout the world, Mr. D's class began writing letters to children in refugee camps. The letters began with short introductions about themselves and then went on to ask the children simple questions such as: What is your name? What is your favorite color? What food do you like to eat? Students believed that allowing children in refugee camps to write about their favorite things and their happiness would allow them to bring to life a small figment of their lives before displacement. Mr. D posted letters that would be sent back to his students around the classroom. He further stated,

> These letters are living artifacts of history in the making. My students have built an intimate bridge to other worlds and have extended the hand of friendship and understanding. This is peace education in my world. Every time a letter arrives it feels like a grand celebration. I think we are celebrating humanity, dignity and compassion in its most organic form. These activist projects were not drawn from a textbook, but rather they were developed from student reflection, creativity and their sense of ownership over their understanding about human tragedy. This is not memorizing facts for a test ... this is real for them.

This activist peace project created an intimate space for global friendship, understanding and empathy for his class. Developing a personal connection and "bearing witness" to the realities of violence in its various manifestations alters the mundane task of merely analyzing historical images with prescribed questions on a worksheet. Mr. D's classroom poses real possibilities for critical peace pedagogy in that he insists that his students be authentic in their analysis, reflection and understanding. Collectively, these narratives from the elementary and middle school classroom provide us with an important understanding of the manner "peace education" is recast within classroom contexts. These teacher activists bring historical moments into the present and through this lens encourage their students to symbolically interrupt contemporary forms of violence. Given the volatile social climate, teachers are increasingly being found to resist engaging in the difficult conversations.

It will, however, become inevitable to address issues of violence as racist forms are surfacing in the schoolyard playground. Young children are verbalizing what they hear in the media and popular culture and are targeting their peers. Verbal bullying and racial slurs are merely being handled on a case by case basis and are not being addressed in curriculums nor in the classroom. School climate has been documented to play a key role in fostering a sense of belonging and garnering self-esteem for students. As political and global violence continue to take place, schools become the site where these forms become reproduced. Interrupting them is oftentimes the task of school officials. Are there effective policies in place that can prevent bullying to further foster peaceful school environments? The DASA Act or The Dignity for All Students Act in New York represents one attempt to do so. It has been criticized, nevertheless, for being merely words on paper. In the following chapter, I explore the various frameworks that have been put in place to keep the conversation alive around the DASA Act, and further how this has served to bolster or hinder student led initiatives to develop peaceful school environments.

4

DIGNITY FOR ALL STUDENTS ACT AND CRITICAL PEACE ACTIVISM

> We must take sides. Neutrality helps the oppressor, never the victim.
> Silence encourages the tormentor, never the tormented.
>
> —Elie Wiesel

Both boys looked at one another in the discipline office. Andrew had ripped off Gian's turban in school. This was the third time it had happened. Andrew had been in detention before and was not fazed by his visit to the discipline office. Gian was traumatized. Andrew's behavior only exemplified Gian's feelings of not belonging in the school and his own fears of being called a terrorist and being told that he should be sent back to his country. Andrew was forthright in his attitude and told the discipline dean, "I don't like Gian. I don't like that rag on his head. His people are dangerous and don't belong in America! This is the truth and nothing will change my mind". The Dean looked at Andrew and simply said, "Andrew, that is inappropriate talk and we all get along here in this school. We all come here to learn". With that, Andrew was again asked to stay afterschool in detention. Andrew apologized to Gian, yet it was obvious that the deep-seated hate and violent behavior had not been touched upon, nor had Gian's feelings of rejection and helplessness addressed. This was business as usual as countless policies and discipline plans fail to sustain or transform the culture of schools.

Reflecting on the work of elementary students in the previous chapter, it was not until Selena and Saira made segregation relevant in their elementary classrooms that it became truly addressed and disrupted. The answers and solutions to the cultures of violence in schools remain to be discovered and limited gains allow for the persistence of it. As stated by the school administrator that "we come here to learn" only further exacerbates forms of

Dignity for All Students Act and Critical Peace Activism **65**

violence and are certainly learned, are normalized and rarely interrupted. History tells us that uninterrupted violence in schools can escalate to murder such as schoolyard shootings. In particular, the incident of the Marcelo Lucero murder case in Long Island became the focal point for discussion in my own classroom.

The Marcelo Lucero murder case and the racial tensions around it became intimately tied to conversations that took place in my classroom. In 2008, seven high school students decided one evening that they would go "beaner hopping" or "get a Mexican". This had become a violent sport for these students, and they were conducting these violent acts weekly. In 2008, the violent sport turned fatal as the seven boys murdered Marcelo Lucero, an Ecuadorean immigrant who was returning home from the local train station. Treated as a hate crime, three of the perpetrators were sentenced to multi-year jail terms for the hate crime. During a discussion on the targeting of undocumented day laborers and rising racial tensions in Long Island, students were challenging their own viewpoints about racism and segregation that they had experienced in their high schools. A general consensus in the classroom about bullying was also being addressed. For the most part, students agreed that the majority of conflict and violence was curtailed on a superficial basis. A student raised her hand and stunned the classroom with her confession:

> I went to school with the seven boys involved in the Lucero case. They seemed to be your everyday high school students. In our school it was obvious that there were 'race wars'. It was White against Latino for the most part. It was normal school stuff to have groups against each other. Then the murder happened. It was shocking and it was wrong. But what made me begin to question everything was when I would hear parents, teachers and other students sympathize with the boys who murdered that man, and even the fact that people cried when the boys were sentenced and were angry and thought they should be let free. It makes you wonder about the value we give to life and with the attitudes at the school, how can you ever turn the violence around that starts with everyday bullying.

There was a moment of pause in the classroom as we bore witness to this confession. After a long pause, one student responded, "Looking back, how might have things been different? Could the violence have been stopped?" I reminded the class that this was a very important question to ask and in order to look forward we must look back. After a rigorous discussion, it became clear that the general concern amongst the students was centered on the need to uphold the dignity of each individual, yet the roadmap to get there was unclear.

Schools are not immune to the violence in society and more often than not become the sites that reverberate political, social and cultural forms. Schools are a far cry from being beacons of safety, acceptance and peace. School climate is a key component of peace curriculum, as messages are sent to learners about what and who matters. As a microcosm of greater society and the world, complicated forms of violence and power are reproduced. Prejudice, targeting, hate and bias together push learners to disengage and further the failure to interrupt such forms is complacency and subtle affirmation of such oppression. Unsettled emotions about difference lead to the profiling and targeting of students. There is a deep sense of vulnerability for students in schools based on their numerous identity markers such as disability, sexual orientation and ethnicity. In the past 15 years, there has been a steady rise in scrutiny and hate in larger society towards groups that are being profiled and attacked. For example Muslim, Middle Eastern and South Asian Sikh youth face insurmountable backlash after the 2015 Paris attacks as similar to 9/11. The 2016 deadly massacre at a gay nightclub in Florida only further revealed the fear that LGBT youth live with on a daily basis. These incidents become increasingly divisive as they are occupied and utilized by politicians as a policy platform to reinforce whom to "fear" and "hate" in our communities. Mobilizations around hate and fear further trickle down into everyday school life. In a concerted effort to pass legislation to address issues of bullying, New York State presented the Dignity for All Students Act.

The concept of human dignity is powerful and the Dignity for All Students Act in theory symbolized a powerful step in a positive direction. In response to failures of anti-bullying legislation, New York State developed the DASA Act that went into full implementation in 2010 and put forth the requirement of all professionals to be trained on the Act and on bullying as well as require each school to have a DASA coordinator.

The DASA Act aimed to provide the following:

> Instruction in civility, citizenship and character education—Commissioner's Regulations 100.2(c): For all public schools, required instruction will be expanded to include, but not be limited to, awareness and sensitivity to harassment and discrimination within the protected classes, identified in the legislation as those who are subjected to intimidation or abuse based on actual or perceived race, color, weight, national origin, ethnic group, religion, religious practice, disability sexual orientation, gender or sex.

With legislation as the DASA Act in place, schools are held accountable by law to interface, prevent and follow up on acts of bullying. Every teacher and school staff member is required to take a DASA training program and schools allocate an individual who becomes the point person for bullying incidents. Character programs have been implemented to reinforce the ideas of the Dignity Act and

Dignity for All Students Act and Critical Peace Activism **67**

to normalize zero tolerance policies into the fabric of school culture. Despite the efforts on paper, however, the DASA Act has largely contributed to superficial acknowledgement of issues of race, hate and bias in schools. The DASA Act requires schools to document and report cases of bullying annually, and not surprisingly, schools have overwhelmingly reported zero incidents in their schools. This data strikes one as unreal, or that with little implementation, bullying has suddenly been curbed. On the other hand, it simply reinforces the reality that school districts embrace their positioning as affluent, good schools and to admit that issues of racism, homophobia, sexism and Islamophobia (to name a few) exist within their schools would be to tarnish the very reputations that have been built alongside exclusive, segregationist housing policies. Within these districts, as has been argued in previous chapters, diversity is tokenized as a box to check off during the school year with the yearly diversity and wear your ethnic clothes to school day. Despite the resistance to fully implement the full frameworks of the Dignity Act, I would like to highlight the work of individuals that are determined to make issues of bullying and racism an ongoing dialogue in schools. Their work again becomes the "unofficial" work of peace advocates. It would seem that with the bolstering of the DASA Act, schools could become spaces of activism, critical dialogue and peace. Curriculum in the classroom could potentially be aligned with inquiry and interrogation of histories and silenced voices. Yet lessons on dignity and human rights continue to be realized in merely "unofficial" ways, separate from the core curriculum in schools.

An Act of Bullying: An Act of Genocide

There has been an unprecedented rise in hate crimes and Islamophobia in the past year since the terrorist attacks on Paris in 2015. Communities have been experiencing the backlash as well as students in their school buildings. Mother Jones magazine recently published an article entitled, "The Chilling Rise of Islamophobia in our Schools" (Jan 26, 2016). In this article, they report the following:

> The reports of threats and attacks are on the rise in schools across the United States, too. A seventh grader in Vandalia, Ohio, threatened to shoot a Muslim boy on the bus ride home from school, calling him a "towel head," a "terrorist," and "the son of ISIS." A sixth grade girl wearing a hijab in the Bronx was reportedly punched by three boys who called her "ISIS." Even before Paris and San Bernardino, a 2014 survey by the Council on American Islamic Relations found that 52 percent of Muslim students in California reported being the target of verbal abuse and insults. That's double the number of students who report being bullied based on gender and race nationwide.

68 Dignity for All Students Act and Critical Peace Activism

> What's most distressing to the council is how many anti-Muslim incidents have started with a teacher or a school administrator, as was the case with 14-year-old Ahmed Mohamed, who was arrested after he brought a clock to his school in Texas.

These are deeply distressing statistics and are similar to the experience of Sikh and Muslim youth post 9/11 and presently as well. Student run organizations can be the most powerful force to counteract hate in schools, especially when teachers and administrators struggle with their response to bigotry and hate. The article also advocates for greater presence of diverse voices and ethnic histories in schools. For example, Karanveer Singh Pannu, a high school student in New Jersey, has also created his own book on bullying against Sikh children. Daily, we are reminded of the struggles that vulnerable youth are faced with and the manner they are fighting their battles alone. When there is a strong correlation with global events and a rise in bullying towards targeted groups, it requires one to take pause and think deeply about how to interrupt racist forms that are making schools places of violence and apathy.

In the current moment, we are also faced with an added burden, The Trump Effect. When individuals like Donald Trump are marked as heroes in young children's minds, racist forms can become legitimized and sadly applauded. As I had previously written about in earlier chapters, social movements are powerful and counterhegemonic resistance faces up against very influential bigoted mobilizations that are gaining legitimacy. When they gain legitimacy, their messages become "safe" or acceptable regardless of however racist they may be. For example, it was recently reported in Vice News by Daniel Hernandez that:

> In northwest Indiana last week, Trump's face was used by a group of "super fan" students at a predominantly white Catholic high school in northwest Indiana to taunt students at a rival Catholic school that is mostly Latino. The white students also chanted, "Build a wall!", referencing Trump's campaign pledge to build a wall on the border with Mexico. (March 2016)

A similar incident took place in Des Moines Iowa where students were chanting "Trump Trump" and "mini Mexico" against rival teams. These incidents are taking place at colleges as well. As was reported by Inside Higher Ed on March 15, 2016 two Northwestern University students have been charged with vandalizing a chapel on campus with spray paint, writing a swastika, slurs against black and gay people—and the word "Trump". Days later, two students at Wichita State University—one Muslim and one Hispanic—were attacked at a gas station by a man who shouted, "Trump, Trump, Trump, we will make America great again. You losers will be thrown out of the wall".

The Southern Poverty Law Center additionally published a report entitled *"The Trump Effect: The Impact of The Presidential Campaign on Our Nation's Schools"* in April 2016. The findings of the report paint a grim picture of the growing "normalization" around the politics of hate and xenophobia that has become the platform from which Trump has chosen to mobilize his campaign. Schools as sites of social and cultural reproduction begin to feel the immediate negative impact of such rhetoric especially when there is little effort to interrupt racist forms. The report notes an increase in anxiety and fear amongst students of color while simultaneously noting students who are becoming emboldened and divisive. Some highlighted findings of the report are as follows:

> More than two-thirds of the teachers reported that students—mainly immigrants, children of immigrants and Muslims—have expressed concerns or fears about what might happen to them or their families after the election. More than half have seen an increase in uncivil political discourse. More than one-third have observed an increase in anti-Muslim or anti-immigrant sentiment. More than 40 percent are hesitant to teach about the election.

According to teacher and student commentaries, the report stated the following:

> "Students are hearing more hate language than I have ever heard at our school before", says a high school teacher in Helena, Montana. Another teacher reports that a fifth grader told a Muslim student "that he was supporting Donald Trump because he was going to kill all of the Muslims if he became president!"

The report provides rich data that reinforces the challenges and pressures of "common sense" that is increasingly divisive, stems from racist nativism and clearly contributes to nationalist imaginaries that exclude a large segment of the American populace. Such "nationalist imaginaries" are increasingly based on anti-immigrant rhetoric, Islamophobia and homophobia and built upon a rejection of "Otherness". There is a clear nationalist agenda that is imagined that instills fear, divides communities and rewrites the parameters of belonging. This report brings us back to Benhabib's (2004) arguments that the tensions with "Otherness" is a barrier to nation-states in their abilities to establish codes of belonging, and to negotiate secure boundaries and borders and to establish who belongs. When the data indicates that children as young as kindergarten are able to vocalize fear or participate in hate, it only becomes another indication of the profound and urgent need to interrupt and forge a counter-narrative and counter-hegemonic dialogue. I am highlighting these incidents in particular, not to say that racism begins and ends with

Trump's rise to popularity, but rather to illustrate the incredible swiftness with which the larger political climate and events, permeate and become part of school settings.

A critical counter voice and acts of interruption are rare and further the failure to interrupt these forms leads to their flourishing. It is a clear failure on the part of educators to be activists and a clear indication about how schools continue to mirror and mimic society—to the extent of mimicry of blatant racist rhetoric from presidential candidates. Trump solicits membership in his group by denigrating others, by similarly denigrating, one seeks membership where he is the leader and he preys on people's desire to belong and to be part of a group, therefore you push others out to gain entry and acceptance. Trump has been lauded as a "gateway drug" to bring together formally estranged white supremacist and conservative groups together. Such mobilization is dangerous, and more so when it leads to everyday acts of bullying and targeting amongst the youngest members of our society. Quite contrary, to popularly held beliefs, bullying is not a "normal" part of growing up and recognizing that is crucial. It is yet another reminder of how far we reside from realizing peace and humanizing pedagogy despite the presence of legal responsibility via the DASA Act. But we don't throw the towel in for the difficult work of humanization must continue.

Similar to the need to go beyond the official curriculum and official practice in schools, many organizations are embracing the charge to implement, reinforce and keep the conversations alive in relation to student dignity. The "unofficial" work of these individuals is important to highlight as we have quickly come to realize that the DASA Act has again become words on paper, with little sustained impact.

Genocide and Bullying

> ... an incident of bullying can lead to a genocide. Beth Lilach, Senior Director of Education and Community Affairs from the Holocaust Memorial and Tolerance Center

Advocates from the Holocaust Center in Long Island tirelessly educate in schools and universities in the local area in order to keep the conversation going about bullying, hate and genocide. Beth Lilach, the Senior Director of Education and Community Affairs, reminds us that perhaps we tread dangerous waters. Annually, Beth Lilach works with youth to adults to open up the uncomfortable discussions about the Holocaust and the politics of hate that lead to its development. She believes that one moment of conflict can quickly escape us and escalate to a genocide and we then must discover how we can open up such dialogue in our classrooms. Similar to arguments previously stated, allowing students to develop their own historical post memory lens brings it closer to home and allows them to participate and understand that they have a stake in the progression of history. Using the Holocaust as a point of departure, students are taken on a journey back to the escalation of genocides and are encouraged to ask questions about the historic atrocities. Questions that are posed to students are oftentimes framed in ways that encourage critical analysis as well as situating the learner in the position to reflect with present day genocides and xenophobia as a lens. Lilach was holding back tears as she spoke about events which she has studied for 23 years. Two decades of hyper-exposure to the Holocaust's atrocities haven't jaded her; it is a history she can feel, she said, especially when survivors visit to share their stories. "To be with people of historical value-it's not just history any more", said Lilach.

As stated in the a local newspaper,

> "Under the Nazi regime, it became a crime to be compassionate and through the Tolerance Center, Beth Lilach works to change the culture of schools as administration does its part to implement the DASA Act. When there is nationalized news of hate crimes and murders Beth Lilach works with law enforcement and to encourage them to constantly be aware of morality and authority. Lilach asserts that we must be teaching tolerance to improve the human condition." Cushman said.
>
> The cadets were part of an innovative program run by the Holocaust Memorial and Tolerance Center of Nassau County that teaches police cadets about tolerance through the Holocaust. The 4-hour program is mandatory for all cadets in the Nassau police academy and the Suffolk County police force has recently made the program mandatory. The day's program begins with an overview about the Holocaust, followed by a tour of the museum and meetings with survivors. Afterwards, the students partake in a discussion run by a member of the Anti-Defamation League.

Beth Lilach educates widely to youth about the history of the Holocaust while paralleling acts in US history that demonstrate how the failure to act can lead to greater atrocities. She also speaks about how everyday bullying is a first step in the making of genocide. Lilach reminds students that "the hate of others and the desire to rid society of those you do not like is similar to the feelings during the Holocaust". Yet Beth Lilach makes the point that genocide is a choice. Such a statement counters the assumptions that are made by many that the Holocaust just happened by force for all participants. Through her assertions students are reminded that our words and thoughts that are connected to hate can have greater consequences. Lilach dispels the many myths surrounding these atrocities that genocides don't happen overnight. They begin somewhere and can that "somewhere" be interrupted? As a peace advocate and activist,

72 Dignity for All Students Act and Critical Peace Activism

Beth Lilach shared the following personal thoughts on the DASA Act and its implementation.

> In August 2007, only a few weeks after I began working at the Holocaust Memorial and Tolerance Center, I received my first call for an anti-bullying program. The request came from the principal of a Jewish school who had a severe bullying problem in the Kindergarten class. I should not have been surprised, but I was. Over the years, I conducted countless anti-bullying and tolerance classes for parents, teachers, college students, and middle and high school students. As someone who was abused by fellow students in elementary and junior high (middle) school, I felt hopeful in 2011, when I first learned of DASA going into effect on July 1, 2012. I hoped that the State and the DOE were becoming proactive and more serious against the increasing incidents of bully and cybercide. On paper, DASA sounded good. In reality, I believed it was doomed to failure because the State was not offering financial or administrative support to schools. I also did not understand how the new policies were to be implemented and enforced. The way that I interpreted DASA, was that schools were left to self-report and self-solve. There did not seem to be any further action by the State regarding the reports. I did not see any tangible process of follow-up or repercussions for bullying incidents.
>
> In the summer 2012, I began to receive requests from school districts to provide staff training on the new DASA Act. I created a special power point presentation to conduct at schools called "Dignity Act for Faculty and Staff: The Holocaust as Touchstone for Understanding New York's Anti-Harassment Legislation". I presented the program to several schools in Nassau County during the summer and fall 2012. The audiences included school nurses, guidance counselors, bus drivers, janitorial staff, and administrators.
>
> My presentation did explain DASA, but the actual Act was only superficially examined. The topics that were discussed in depth were: Choices during Extreme Prejudice, Choices during Bullying and Prejudice, Legal and Moral Choices.
>
> In October 2011, I added a new term to my presentation–bullycide. It was heartbreaking to teach parents that a new word had been coined to describe suicide committed by young people who had been acutely bullied by peers. Relentless and brutal bullying is better defined as "abuse". The word "bullying" has become a euphemism which no longer accurately describes the sadism, emotional violence, and all the various forms of abuse (physical, sexual, social, psychological, cyber) that some students experience. In many unfortunate cases, parents, teachers, and law enforcement have dismissed bullying as harmless or a rite of childhood. Labeling the victimization as "abuse" sometimes facilitates action by parents and officials.

Beth Lilach provides us with an honest analysis of the shortcomings of the DASA act and coupled with her keen awareness of the rising incidents of bullying and hate crimes, it is counterintuitive to accept reports of zero incidents of bullying in school districts after DASA. Beth Lilach continues to extend her critical work to issues of gender and the distinct ways women are abused and exploited during acts of war. The New York Times on March 10, 2016 reported on the exhibit that is on display at the Center in the article entitled, "Women, Not Victims: Moving Beyond Sexualized Atrocities During Genocide". In the article written by journalist Aileen Jacobson, Beth Lilach further elaborates on aspects of the gender based atrocities. For example, in the article she states that "children of the rape victims were often "used for pseudo-experiments to 'prove' white supremacist ideology", and further "This is a topic that has generally been overlooked and trivialized", even by genocide scholars and historians. A few academic conferences have addressed the subject in recent years but it's still cutting edge". Survivors have often felt stigmatized or shamed, she said, and women have rarely been in positions to bring public attention to the acts that mostly plague women and girls.

Facing History Facing Ourselves and the Holocaust

Former senior program associate with Facing History Facing Ourselves, Tracy Garrison-Feinberg has brought her expertise as well to the Holocaust Memorial and Tolerance Center and is the Director of Claire Friedlander Education Institute. She is responsible for education programs for elementary through high school, as well as professional development for teachers at those levels. Below I have documented her answers related to my exploration of her work.

RV: Describe the work you do with schools related to DASA and supporting positive school climates; How do you use history and work with the Holocaust center to address everyday acts of bullying?

TRACY: HMTC has been offering tolerance and anti-bullying programming for a number of years now, both at the Center and at individual schools, from fourth through twelfth grades. All of our programming for students emphasizes the choices that individuals and groups make, historically and today. When students come to the Center for a field trip and museum tour, we begin by asking them to reflect on roles people took on in the history of the Holocaust: perpetrator, collaborator, bystander, upstander, victim/target. We emphasize that each role had choices, except that of victim/target. By having young people reflect on these roles historically, they can also think about times in their own lives where they move through these roles, and the decision making behind those choices. We also have developed specific anti-bullying programming and tolerance & awareness workshops that allow for small group discussion about these roles in contemporary situations.

74 Dignity for All Students Act and Critical Peace Activism

RV: How does your previous work with Facing History help you in your approach to DASA?

TRACY: At Facing History, the primary focus was on the choices people make and helping students understand how to be better critical thinkers. Making the connections between identity, membership, and historical events shaped my approach to a number of historical case studies, and I've worked to bring that philosophy to my work here at HMTC, where it complements the original mission of HMTC: to teach the history of the Holocaust and its lessons through education and community outreach. We teach about the dangers of antisemitism, racism, bullying and all other manifestations of intolerance. We promote resistance to prejudice and advocate respect for every human being.

RV: How do you define dignity (as the title is Dignity for all Students Act)?

TRACY: I define dignity as the recognition of humanity in all people; the imperative to treat everyone with respect. Basically, it is to take the Golden Rule to heart and put it into practice—to treat everyone the way I expect to be treated.

RV: What are some of the challenges you are facing with DASA in terms of follow through and long lasting change?

TRACY: It's more of a concern than a challenge—I hope that by implementing DASA and establishing coordinators and programming in schools across New York, that communities are truly committing to promoting respect for each and every student, in each and every student. I hope DASA doesn't become just another part of the wallpaper but that schools think about what it means for their communities in particular, and that they work every day to uphold the spirit as well as the letter of DASA. Ultimately we want every single student to feel safe enough in their school environment for learning to happen. I also hope that DASA doesn't become limited to just a few targeted groups in its implementation: while LGBTQ+ teens are at particular risk, that we understand that DASA will work best when we acknowledge that every single student is worthy of respect, and that this is ongoing work. One assembly per year will not do it justice. And while bullying is one of the most obvious manifestations of intolerance at schools, DASA should be about more than bullying—it does and should have implications for civil and human rights locally and globally, including migration and refugee issues, gender relations, etc.

RV: Do you believe DASA can be effective in addressing the issues of bullying?

TRACY: Yes, if educators and other adults take it seriously, and model the Dignity Act in their own behavior.

"Silence is acceptance—speak loudly". Alisty

Alisty Joy Keneth has been a key figure in local area advocacy and development of legislation and school programs. Alisty is a leading community advocate and activist in Long Island and presents us with additional understanding of how hate crimes and bias have continued to be a presence regardless of legislation such as the DASA Act. She has continuously advocated for the implementation of the big lessons that directly relate to the DASA Act and how schools can utilize these great messages to foster an environment of belonging and safety and the free expression of self. Through the past several years Alisty continues to understand that schools have far to go in order to realize communities of peace and global citizenship.

In 1999, Alisty lobbied for the NYS Hate Crimes legislation, which led to the development of assistance to victims of hate crimes and the education of the public about hate crimes in the local and state judicial system. After 9/11, there was a shift in the occurrence of hate crimes. Hate crimes that were largely based on homophobia in addition to targeting the Latino population became concentrated around Islamophobia. The targeted populations were largely Middle Eastern, Sikh and Muslim. In 2007, she created an educational institute that provided advocacy and awareness about the hate crimes legislation and most importantly she worked diligently to educate targeted populations about the new law.

Alisty stated that:

> The environment of hate and prejudice is quite dependent on the political climate—different targets fall victim to hate crimes, it is a moving radar. Previously, I was educating people in gay straight coffee shops and that changed to my presence in temples and gurdwaras and mosques. I made it my responsibility to educate them about their rights and how they are protected by law. They needed to know about the frameworks about what entails a hate crime—and whether the motivation bias or prejudice?

Alisty was keenly aware of growing resistance to the influx of South Asian youth in schools that were previously predominately white. On the heels of 9/11 it created a dynamic that she believed was in need of interruption. With highly segregated school districts by social class, as is the case with Long Island, upwardly mobile communities have moved into previously white affluent communities. In some instances, the "model minority" stereotypes were utilized to gain acceptance within these communities. Alisty noted that this dynamic shifted after 9/11,

> I could see a shift in hate and bias in schools because of the increase in brown students being targeted in Nassau county, NY. Suddenly the brown kids were taking over the scholarships—it became the model minority wrapped up in Islamophobia—the smart brown kids were labeled as infiltrating and they were positioned as Al Qaeda. Nobody was interrupting the discourse, because it was assumed that the brown kids will be okay. But wait a minute, it is not okay.

76 Dignity for All Students Act and Critical Peace Activism

For the past decade, Alisty has worked towards opening up the dialogue about hate and bias and prejudice reduction. Her work focuses on both the victims and victimizers, and through numerous in class activities and presentations her message is influential. She is not romantic about it, however, and realizes how we have mostly remained stagnant in our attempts to move beyond the barriers of prejudice. Similar to the response by Beth Lilach, Alisty also has her reservations about the ability of DASA to make long lasting change. She stated the following:

> Once DASA came out everyone wanted to do Diversity–it became fashionable to have diversity with your mix it up day and student courts and multicultural awareness day—but it remains to be a superficial engagement with the issues. Hate and bias are not feel good things—they are very serious and take lives.

Alisty believes that in order for DASA to be effective it needs reworking.

> DASA or dignity should be an ongoing dialogue and we need it in the curriculum. It should be something schools deal with every day. It has been largely ineffective—obviously the conversations students hear such as the hate and bias from political candidates who are putting thing out there is on their minds. Nobody is talking about it. We want to believe it is 'we are the world holding our hands' for one day and 364 days the conversations is on the back burner.

She further concluded:

> Things are not occurring in a vacuum and the counter voice is very weak to what students are hearing and seeing every day. Resistance continues to be isolated.
>
> What needs to happen is to make DASA more than a symbolic moment—we need grassroots activism. We use the title "Dignity for all students Act" but what needs to happen is to reach those students that become undignified—or whose dignity is stolen from them—the marginalized. DASA act activities usually are for the feel good people and the effects of these superficial enactments are good for those that are the cream of the crop. Doing dignity should not just stop at being a college resume builder. Currently, from what I can notice–the same students are the ones that attend human rights conferences and do diversity awareness and it is largely for either status, obligation or for recognition— rather than the realization of those rights for others—that is where the work needs to be done.

DASA, for the large part has failed to address the needs of students according to activists that have their finger on the pulse of social climates in schools. Sadly, school districts skirt around DASA and its true implementation, perhaps to resist a true diagnosis of the challenges they may face in their schools.

> Anything related to rights, hate, bias, peace right now is the 'in my own backyard mentality'. If it doesn't directly relate to you and your world, it's not on your radar. DASA is a very nice wrapping on a box—but it is giftwrap on an empty box. There is no reporting of incidents and no one is speaking about it. At the end of the day, school districts don't want to be labeled racists, therefore there is no reporting.

In terms of the teacher audience that she hopes to work with, Alisty felt that teachers are a product of the times they live in. She believed that there is a difference in the audience when teachers are a product of the 1970s because she notices that they live the ideology of human rights. Currently, she believes, teacher activists are few and far between and those that do act are resisted by their colleagues and the larger community. Most importantly, however, is that dedicated peace activists continue to seek out the spaces where their work can be done. As is the case with the larger agenda of this book, these activist identities deserve notice.

Teacher activists play a central role in inculcating lessons on peace praxis. What might it look like if we were to make critical peace education a central facet of teacher preparation? Oftentimes, discussions related to violence in the world and the lives of students are relegated to sparse readings on urban education or an analysis of segregation and Brown vs. Board of Education. When we solely rely on court cases such as Brown vs. Board of Education as evidence of an integrated and non-violent society and equitable schools, we fail ourselves greatly. The battles are far from won. It is only when pre-service teachers are empowered to understand the ongoing nature of violence, oppression and injustice in society and schools that we may explore strategies of disruption. Teachers in training represent a key group of individuals that could potentially transform their classroom spaces and enact coalitions within their schools to take matters of violence seriously. Understanding how violence interrupts lives could ideally further become incorporated into the fabric of school pedagogies. In the following chapter, the context of peace education in pre-service teacher education courses will be visited.

5

CRITICAL PEACE PEDAGOGUES—
SHAPING TEACHERS IN TRAINING

> Liberation is thus a childbirth, and a painful one. The man or woman who emerges is a new person, viable only as the oppressor-oppressed contradiction is superseded by the humanization of all people. Or to put it another way, the solution of this contradiction is born in the labor which brings into the world this new being: no longer oppressor nor longer oppressed: but human in the process of achieving freedom.
>
> —Freire p. 49 *Pedagogy of the Oppressed*

Teachers Working Through Privilege

Every semester, I look around my classroom filled with anxious teachers in training. "Why do you want to become a teacher?" I ask this question. Responses typically are "I love children", "Teaching is a noble profession", "I come from a family of teachers, that's all I know" and even "I was told teaching would be a good choice for me". In pre-service teacher education courses, students arrive with high expectations on being trained "to teach". Where would you like to teach? Students would then go on to state, "I have an opportunity where I went to school". "I really want to teach in the school district where I grew up". "As long as I don't have to go to the 'city' I will be happy". With full admiration that my students have decided to pursue teaching, I commend them, yet I become the bearer of troubling news, that "loving children" is not the ideal reason to teach and teaching in the schools where they grew up only serves to reproduce systems that exclude and discriminate many segments of society. Teaching is complex, deeply engaging work, and is a serious commitment to challenge the status quo. Teaching requires innovation and conviction about educating students from all walks of life. Beginning teachers need to be encouraged to understand and to contextualize what is around them and further to be wary of merely reproducing social inequalities around them. I am never alarmed when students respond with silence, roll their eyes and offer me blank stares. Yet, from time to time there will be a student who proclaims, "I want to make a difference and I welcome the challenge to teach in a high needs district" or "The call to teachers is to always be better and do better than those that came before them". It is a reminder to me, however, that teacher activists are intrinsically shaped by their life experiences and those individuals that are determined to engage in meaningful pedagogical work will do so despite circumstances.

There is a widespread assumption by new students that given the correct lesson plan and proper execution, teaching takes place. The educator is merely the lesson plan executor. Critiqued by Freire, the banking method of teaching and learning is increasingly viewed as the task of teachers. According to Freire, "There are innumerable well-intentioned bank-clerk teachers who do not realize that they are serving only to dehumanize" (1997 p. 56). Given the growing reliance on numbers in the certification process to gain a teaching license, effective teaching has become progressively quantifiable and measurable. Thus, with the expectation that they will be trained to achieve the desired numerical evaluation to be granted a license, students are overwhelmingly narrowly focused. Oversimplification or a paint by numbers model of teaching is dangerous. With the attitude that they are only required to teach the test, they walk away from curriculum that veers away from this prime focus.

Peace education is a pie in the sky and the most unlikely concern on their minds. If peace education were to somehow make its way into a pre-service classroom, it would be minimized to a check the box activity. "Peace education" is also highly compartmentalized in a toolkit fashion. To gain further insight, we can evaluate the relevance of Edward Brantmeier's (2011 p. 356) stages of critical peace education that he defines for teacher education: (1) raising consciousness through dialogue; (2) imagining nonviolent alternatives; (3) providing specific modes of empowerment; (4) transformative action; (5) reflection and re-engagement (Bajaj 2015). Brantmeier states that "rather than status quo reproduction, critical peace education aims to empower educators as transformative change agents" (Freire 1972) who critically analyze race, class and gender oppression alongside their students and who provide culturally responsive pedagogy, culturally inclusive curriculum and fair assessment of diverse learners. Merely teaching a "social justice" scripted curriculum, however, does not necessarily elicit a political act. In my pre-service classroom, students are positioned to confront ideological frameworks and are provided with an understanding of the multiple forms of systemic

80 Critical Peace Pedagogues—Shaping Teachers in Training

violence that shape education. Students are told from the first day of class that they will not be taught how to teach, but rather that they will gain a greater understanding of the multiple hegemonic frameworks that they must navigate and disrupt in order to make an impact and become activists. Yes, I am guilty of an agenda and it is an agenda to complicate students' ways of thinking about themselves and their students to become "activists" and critical agents of possibility and not merely "passive" consumers of knowledge succumbed to complacency.

With the understanding that the majority of our teachers in training are embedded in privilege and power, can we draw them in to be allies and activists? Are there the "in between moments" that can be occupied by a politics of interruption and resistance? Can critical peace pedagogy permeate classroom discussions as normalized discourse and as essential components of teacher education? As Freire so rightly asserts, the journey for the oppressor to understand their position of power can be likened to childbirth and through the anguish the oppressor must become human and participate in the liberation of the oppressed. To approach the idea of privilege and understanding one's relation to it, teacher and student alike tread an unpredictable landscape. By virtue of one's moment of birth, one has experienced privilege or lack of it, and in place of accusatory rhetoric or finger blaming–there exist spaces to open dialogue about the meaning of entitlement. Where does dehumanization take place and how it is interrupted? There is much written about privilege, Whiteness and the great disconnect that rightly exists between the homogeneity of the teacher workforce and its lack of alignment with diverse populations. This has been well documented in the literature. There is great consensus that a mere course on diversity falls short of truly realizing the urgency of understandings of institutionalized discourses of oppression.

Questions about dominant forms of power should ideally arise at the early onset of an academic program and continue to be revisited throughout. The idea of teachers as peace activists or agents of humanization is an important one to flesh out. According to Freire (1997), "nobody educates anybody else, nobody educates himself, people educate each other through their interactions with the world". The role of the teacher is to problematize and demand that our students have a direct participation in their world. How can educators be challenged to encourage students to form themselves rather than be formed? The first moment of inquiry requires a rigorous understanding of personal biases and beliefs that lead to a critical lens. In order for a teacher to attain a level of empathy and compassion with their students, it requires a process. Teacher education programs bear the responsibility of developing each segment of this process. As an essential component of peace education, unofficial lessons on experiencing "dehumanization" through role play and discussion, for example, can serve to open up this dialogue.

The Teacher as Peace Activist: Agents of Humanization

At what moment can we declare that becoming an educator requires one to become a peace activist, a transformative individual and an advocate for humanization? Is there a charge to do so? There is a vast difference in understanding in regard to how good teacher preparation is defined and further who can be considered a highly qualified teacher. Teacher education programs can be guilty as charged as they oftentimes lack any meaningful engagement with issues of oppression, exploitation and dehumanization. One faces the obvious barriers of individuals who choose to deskill and compartmentalize teacher training–and further individuals who view their responsibility as a future teacher to simply impart information and skill sets. Efforts to embrace critical peace pedagogy and global citizenship again become the personal choice of faculty members to make these issues the foundation of their work and to require that their students are very much immersed within the critical lens of humanizing their pedagogy.

The call to duty of young teachers in training would be to begin with unveiling their inner workings on issues and to uproot their deep-seated belief systems and analyze them with compassion. Compassion instead of pushing guilt upon students in these vulnerable spaces is critical. Further, followed by ongoing self-reflection, students could then be asked to further imagine the openings where they might continue to encourage their own students to be critical and reflective citizens. In order to open spaces of dialogue in regard to issues of privilege and power, it requires a level of commitment and determination to move beyond the barriers. Research tends to view Whiteness and the privilege that comes with it as a barrier. My argument here is that it is easy to compartmentalize the notion of white privilege and to call out on pre-service teachers as in need of "treatment" or immersion in understandings of their privilege; to undo their lens. Perhaps, in place of "undoing" their lens, we might view it as broadening their worldview and incorporating elements of self-reflection.

Such self-reflection comes with empathy and requires an understanding that we can have one foot deeply set in a privileged realm and the other can be unprivileged as we simultaneously can wear multiple hats. At any one moment, we can all be guilty of being situated in a realm of power and privilege. For example, I may be an out gay male living in an upper class neighborhood, yet I am targeted, bullied and I live a life in hiding. I am a poor Jewish woman from an urban neighborhood and I have privilege. I am a Sikh American in an affluent neighborhood to much extent as a South Asian I have embraced the model minority label–and am clearly upper middle class enjoying the privilege of status and access to power—and suddenly feel the discomfort as I am positioned as a terrorist and am racially profiled. We all simultaneously face the slippery slope of privilege and nationhood and fragmented belonging. And as I am constantly

82 Critical Peace Pedagogues—Shaping Teachers in Training

reminded, the process to transformation is riddled with setbacks, and false starts bell hooks poignantly provides us with an example of this relationship

> White women and black men have it both ways … They can act as oppressor or be oppressed. Black men may be victimized by racism, but sexism allows them to be act as exploiters and oppressors of women. White women might be victimized by sexism, but racism enables them to act as exploiters and oppressors of black people … As long as these two groups or any group, defines liberation as gaining equality with ruling class white men, they have a vested interest in the continued exploitation of others.
>
> (hooks 2000 p. 16)

As new teachers in training, reflections on becoming aware and unlearning positions of entitlement and privilege are valuable and sensitive starting points. Unlike an indoctrination or a curriculum on how to do peace, the possibilities of "becoming" an activist should ideally be explored within mutual conversations of willing agents. The vision to make pre-service teachers aware about their embeddedness in multiple layers of dominant discourse is a practice in humanization and conscientization with the intention of these ideas being multiplied within their own classrooms. At the same time, educators can develop empathy with students and move forward as a new collective of activists in many arenas—as advocates for transformation. We need to view these practices as acts of empowerment and conscientization or an awakening to how we are all deeply embedded and can be simultaneously oppressor and oppressed in contexts. Perhaps it is at this conjuncture where we can empower teachers to become peace activists in the classroom.

Where Must We Stand?

The self-study and action research approach to teaching practice will provide the basis for my analysis and reflection in this chapter. Reflection is a significant component of self-study and action research (Mills 2003) as it is a powerful way to deconstruct the very self in teacher practice and to know about the self in research and practice as well. Reflective practice in teacher education allows teacher educators to explore how teachers learn by including "I" in an epistemology of reflective practice (Whitehead 2000). Reflective pedagogy helps teachers closely examine current practice and spearhead changes as teacher leaders (Reason and Reason 2007). In other words, self-study means studying one's own practice in its simple term, but its definition varies according to role, practice and purpose (Samaras and Freese 2006)—a practice that lends itself to qualitative inquiry which uses narrative, descriptive approaches to data collection, analysis and refinement. In this chapter I will be highlighting my personal classroom-based narratives from a teacher education program in New York State. This teacher education program serves both the city and suburban schools and students are engaged in observations and student teaching in high needs districts. In this particular teacher preparation program there is no defined multicultural or diversity course. Faculty members inculcate unofficial lessons about power and privilege throughout the program in order to develop a sense of normalcy and urgency about such discourse. The work of Paulo Freire is revisited multiple times, as well as faculty developed lessons and classroom activities that interrupt power and privilege. Conversations and confrontations about privilege arise from courses as vast as methodology, foundations, philosophy and critical literacy.

Society driven oppressive labels, social status and poverty can simultaneously determine social mobility, opportunity and privilege and the following activity exemplifies a confrontation with class based privilege and power. Akintunde (2006) believes that:

> confrontation is an essential element of any class that seeks to deconstruct white racist ideology. We expose students to transformative literature, media, and other materials that invite confrontation and examination of how white power and privilege has been perpetuated through the written and spoken word. (p. 36)

Critical pedagogy, in peace education, refers to the recognition of the universal quality of human suffering (Rorty 1989) and the goal to go beyond the recognition of difference and violence to realize an objective of inclusion. Critical peace pedagogy requires an understanding about the ways oppression and violence are normalized in structural and cultural ways in society, and further foster resistance and realize culturally reflective and socially responsible acts. Classroom exercises can serve as interventions and pedagogies of resistance and hence the flirtation with critical peace pedagogy. Imaginably, there could be countless ways to incorporate resistance into everyday acts in the classroom. Yet again, in reality, spaces of interruption and resistance tend to play out in unofficial curriculums. Let me illustrate some examples of how I have transformed the in-between moments in my syllabus to interrupt dehumanization. These narratives illustrate the moment when teachers begin to view themselves as activists and as key agents of transformation. These students' ideas are challenged about what it means "to teach" as they mutually explore parameters for having an impact and as I invite my students to be equal participants in knowledge inquiry and formation.

Classroom Narratives

At the beginning of every semester, I engage my class in an informal activity that is based on class privilege. It is imperative that teachers understand the symbolic violence that shapes their viewpoints and lives. Students oftentimes

84 Critical Peace Pedagogues—Shaping Teachers in Training

state that they only hope to teach in the district where they grew up and fear teaching "those kids". These forms demand interruption and begin with a serious dialogue about the categorizations of bodies in society. This lens is crafted in order to further understand how we ourselves reproduce these violent ideological frameworks and limit us in our role as critical educators. The following role-play activity helps students visualize and enact how we as a society categorize and label one another based on labels that are prescribed by society. Students are given very few instructions but are asked to own the label they are given. When students walk into the classroom door, they are handed their "identity" card. Time is provided for each student to develop a life story behind the identity they are given and a total 20–25 identity labels are allotted. Below are some examples of descriptors that students developed.

> Student A: My name is Jack, I am a 23-year-old white male and I work at Burger King as a fast food worker. I never completed high school but I have bills to pay and I have to support my family. I have no health insurance, but I work 10 hour shifts at minimum wage.
>
> Student B: My name is Patricia and I am 33 years old and I am a doctor. I attended Ivy League schools and I make good money. I worked hard for what I earned and I enjoy living in an exclusive neighborhood.
>
> Student C: My name is Juan and I am an undocumented day laborer. I wait every day for different odds and ends jobs—I risked my life to come here from Mexico. I work very hard—sometimes the people that hire me don't pay my wages. It makes me feel like a slave—but I know I don't have papers—but I am a human being.
>
> Student D: My name is Blake, I am 40 years old and I am homeless. I used to work on Wall Street. I had the good life. I was fired with the Wall Street meltdown—I could never find another job—I became an alcoholic—I want another chance.
>
> Student E: My name is Mohammed, I am 40 years old and from Pakistan. I was a lawyer back home before I immigrated to America. I could not get a job at the same level of my education and it is expensive to go back to school. I decided to work as a yellow cab driver. It makes good money and I can afford to feed my family. I feel like I have more potential than this.
>
> Student F: My name is Laura, I am 48 years old. I have been unemployed for 2 years. I worked for the same company for 25 years and then they decided to outsource jobs. I have an Associates degree and am too old to get new skills. I was good at my job—and I have not received any call backs from my job search.

After students had an opportunity to create their identity profile, they were instructed to mingle around the classroom. Students introduced themselves to one another and were not given any particular instructions as to how to commiserate and group themselves. Two students in the class were given the role of observers. They were provided the charge of listening and observing keenly to how interactions played out and the manner students congregated based on identities.

> Student Observer A: I found it fascinating how people were making comments about certain groups. For example, the homeless, unemployed and day laborers were sort of shunned and brushed off. One student even commented to the homeless that they had nothing in common and that they would need to move away from their group. The highly educated group stuck together and immediately separated from others. This was really amazing how quickly groups were formed.
> Student Observer B: I decided to chat with the group of students that were pushed away from others—the day laborer, homeless, unemployed, fast food worker and cab driver. I asked them why they might have been pushed away. They unanimously answered that they were considered the underbelly of society and the troublemakers—or the groups that have little sympathy from society for their line of work. They are overworked and underpaid or experienced tragedy that led to unemployment or homelessness. They shared immigrant identities as well.

Students were then instructed to place themselves into neighborhoods based on their likelihood of living within the same community. Students were to develop a narrative around their neighborhoods in regard to their lifestyles and habits. The students organized themselves according to status and income. It was quite telling that students reproduced social and class identities and they were able to echo the social attitudes that might be perceived from their pretend neighborhoods. When asked if individuals from the lower income community could move into the affluent suburban neighborhood, there was a resounding "no" or "never" exclaimed. Reasons to prohibit the lower income group into the affluent community were based on privilege, money, entitlement and social attitudes. One student, acting out their role, stated the following,

> Your people are undocumented, workers, laborers and we are doctors, engineers and politicians. We believe we worked hard to earn this, you will also need to work hard and earn your keep. We cannot relate to each other and you will bring crime to our safe and perfect life.

At the conclusion of the activity, students were asked to form a line of privilege and power as they chose to do so. The students lined up in front my classroom, each holding an identity card in front of them. Students giggled, and shuffled around and looked at one another. The labels on the 25 cards covered a

86 Critical Peace Pedagogues—Shaping Teachers in Training

vast array of occupations and identities from doctor, teacher, fast food service worker, stay at home parent unemployed and undocumented day laborer to homeless. Students placed themselves in a line according to the privilege that they believed they might be afforded in society. Not surprisingly, those that populated the front of the lineup possessed identity cards that belonged to those that would earn more money and hence more power. Students at the opposite end of the line were given identity cards that reflected the working class poor.

This activity was then followed up by an in-depth discussion. In particular, students were asked about how these class fractures in society lead to vastly different educational systems. Students responded that they had aligned themselves according to money, class status and power. From their world view and their understanding about societal attitudes, they understood that privilege and entitlement separated individuals in society.

> Student A: This is reality. People are separated based on money and status and how hard you work.
> Student B: What do you mean how hard you work? The day laborer has to work hard and is oftentimes not paid.
> Student A: Well, you know what I mean. Society will reward the educated. Some people have more privilege. The families in the affluent school district worked hard to earn that—maybe if the blue collar families worked harder—they might also be able to reach that level.
> Student B: That does not make it right.
> Student A: But I have a problem if you are not "legal" or if you did not work hard to get your degree. You don't pay taxes—and you are draining the economy. My parents came here legally as immigrants and worked three or four jobs so I could have a better life!
> Student B: Do you assume all people with high status have gotten there fair and square? It's privilege.
> Student C: I think that is the point we are all arguing here—we need to see how privilege separates us and is fair to some and not others. We have to change this!
> Professor: Do we as a society bear the responsibility to change this? Can we change the system so that the children of the day laborer and blue collar worker attend the same school as the child of the doctor and company CEO?
> Student D: Why?
> Professor: To clarify, you are asking me: Why we need to do anything to change the system of power and privilege that dehumanizes many in society?

This powerful moment, although quite illustrative of the implausible resistance to change that exists, allowed me to further develop the dialogue on how segregation is deeply representative of hegemonic discourse, dehumanization and oppression. It is also revealing in that we expose the truths in thinking about "education" as an entitlement. In order to allow the question of humanization to take notice, I push them further and announce that two babies have been born this very instant, one in a privileged affluent district and the other in a high needs poverty ridden district. I probe further and demand an answer to the following question: "What makes one child or the other better and more worthy of a great education—is it merely by virtue of the moment of birth and where they happen to be?" The blank stares are there, yet one or two students have the courage to say, "It should not matter". And this for me sets the tone for further inquiry throughout the semester and where, despite the assigned textbooks and curricular constraints, I make the choice to take my students to uncomfortable places to understand how we as future teachers become violators of human rights when we label and choose to not see the potential and abilities of every one of our students. We engage in enactments of violence with such teacher behavior. Although the grittiness of the classroom moment can be disconcerting it is critical to interrupt these forms. It is also a reminder to me, that had I not challenged such viewpoints, these students may have never questioned their ideas on power. I also imagine the countless classroom moments that pass by where interruptions never take place.

Throughout the semester students are expected to develop creative and novel ways to discuss class readings. As I remind my students, I entrust them with a critical lens to generate meaningful and thoughtful engagement. As a follow up to readings on class privilege my students developed a creative activity called "Building Kites". Students broke the class up into small groups and provided each group with certain sets of materials. One group was provided glue, glitter, markers, construction paper and other required materials for a kite. One group was provided all of these items minus crayons. One group was given merely crayons and paper, while the final group had merely a bottle of glue. Students then asked the class to do the following:

Your task will be to build a kite and when it is complete to bring it to the front of the room.

As the class went about the activity, the discussion leaders could clearly sense the frustration arising from the groups that had less materials and yet were afforded the same task as those with more. The groups with ample materials were on their way and building beautiful and complete kites. At the end of the activity, groups that had enough materials were able to provide a kite for the discussion leaders. The groups lacking materials were noted to be frustrated and angry—and clearly understood that they were expected to provide the same product as other groups yet had little resources. Students were asked to reflect.

> I was so upset that we were not given enough materials—we knew we would not be able to complete the work. The other groups were not willing to share.

> We had more than enough materials and we built beautiful kites and
> we did it quickly and were able to be creative.

This simple activity created by my students hints at their developing understanding and a desire to encourage discussion amongst their peers about the challenges of unequal distribution of resources. Again, interruptions about power came to life. The goal of empathy building through role-play was encouraging. Other exemplary lessons have sparked heated debates about the role of teachers as change agents and ideas about how to change a broken education system. Students have been asked to create an ideal school model that required democratic representation and representation of diverse populations. At the time of the development of this book, key world events were taking place. Traumatic world events unfolded and many classrooms separated themselves from the global arena. The cocoon-like state may have served to avoid controversy and tragedy, yet I encouraged the opposite as I challenged my students to think of ways to incorporate unofficial lessons into their pedagogy in order to foster global citizenship. Equipping new teachers with the confidence and desire to bring global crises into the classroom discussion is far from easy. What might it look like if pre-service teachers were to be trained in how to see global crises as a very real and valuable opportunity? Is it possible to facilitate creativity and critical lessons in the development of lesson planning curriculum? If we are to make it important, it will come to life.

Global Crises as Everyday Lessons

Repeatedly throughout my classes, I informally engage my students in a *"What would you do in your classroom?"* type of exercise. As was mentioned in previous chapters, the world was experiencing the Syrian migrant crisis and in my classes I asked students to spontaneously develop lesson plans around the issue. In my methods course, students were given the charge to create lesson plan ideas related to the Syrian refugee crisis and the Paris terrorist attacks. As an unofficial lesson in my curriculum, I believed the exercise to be important to demonstrate to students how greatly valuable and relevant global events should be in their everyday classrooms. I was greatly impressed by the quality of critical and engaging work that students developed. Let's take for example, the Syrian refugee crisis. I will share three unique narratives on lesson plans that are focused on a current global crises as well as demonstrate the critical skills that can be gained for the students in the classroom.

Math and the Syrian Refugee Crisis

A pre-service math teacher utilized the Syrian refugee crisis to develop a math lesson that would simultaneously teach math facts and empathy for the struggle

Critical Peace Pedagogues—Shaping Teachers in Training **89**

or refugees. The following is a lesson plan narrative that a student developed for the elementary classroom.

> I plan to begin my lesson by first giving a broad overview about anti-immigrant sentiment in European nations. I plan to divide my students into three groups to participate in my activity. Oftentimes when Syrian refugees make the trip to European nations, they must cross through dangerous waters on small rafts in order to get to their destination. Because of the risk attached to the travel plan, many drown to death before they even reach land. I have set up my classroom to resemble the Mediterranean Sea and the three groups of students will travel in their rafts to make it to their destination, which for many Syrians was Greece. Once they are on their rafts, I will read out different scenarios to them; scenarios that Syrians might have faced on their trip so that students can immerse themselves more into what it was like traveling on those dangerous waters. Along with that, I plan to incorporate Math and Geography skills into the plan. I will give directions to students such as Southwest or Northeast to which they must travel to on their rafts. Doing this will reinforce their geography skills. In terms of math, questions that can be raised include time and distance. For example, simple subtraction skills can be reinforced by asking questions such as if they distance from Syria to Greece is 991 miles and you have traveled 653 miles, how many miles are left? Questions that can be raised about time can include something such as; it takes 48 hours to get to Greece, you have been traveling for 32 hours and 15 minutes, how much more time do you need to travel? I think this lesson plan would not only teach students about the hardships faced as a refugee, but also allow them to see what it is like to travel in such dangerous conditions.

This unusual interdisciplinary activity or proposed "unofficial" lesson has the potential to build up an ongoing dialogue in the class about the refugee crisis. This unique Math based social justice curriculum lends to exciting possibilities in this young educators classroom and will hopefully serve as a starting point for further creative ideas.

Fear and Peace

One student chose a debate discussion multi day format to engage in the topic of fear. The activity is based on a high school level classroom and requires the class to be divided into four groups that would be discussing the following topics: Terrorist Attacks on Paris, Anti-Immigrant Discourse, Black Lives Matter Movement and Police Brutality. Each group is assigned a list of questions to research and discuss. Within each group, students represent diverse points of view related to the topic.

90 Critical Peace Pedagogues—Shaping Teachers in Training

Groups	Paris Attacks	Anti-Immigrant Stance	Black Lives Matter Movement	Police Brutality
Point of View	Parisians, Muslims	Syrians, Parisians, European communities	Black students, police officers	Victims of brutality, police officers
Discussion Questions	What is terrorism? Who is responsible? Why does terrorism happen? Have you ever judged someone unfairly because they are Muslim?	Who are the refugees? What are they escaping? How can this situation end? How would you change this? What would you do if you were a refugee? How should refugees be treated?	How about All Lives Matter? How did this movement begin? Why are people in the movement? How do you feel about the movement? Are police to blame?	Have you experienced racism? Have you had a run-in with the police? Should police wear body cameras? What is racial profiling? Do you know your rights if you are arrested? Was justice served in the court cases?

After a day of discussion and research, the teacher would develop a conversation about fear versus peace. Discussion questions would be as follows:

- Is fear the most basic human emotion?
- How does fear rule the responses of different groups related to your group topic?
- What are major world events that were based on fear? (i.e., Holocaust)
- Has fear lead you to do something that you normally would not do?
- What are you doing to do about these issues to be a peace activist and human rights advocate?

These conversations about fear and peace are powerful and are constantly relevant to global events. Building on this lesson plan, a student in the classroom suggested an in-depth analysis of the topic of fear from the Disney film *Zootopia* that was released in 2016. Allowing elementary age students to analyze fear and prejudice through popular film could potentially serve as a powerful platform for larger discussions. As consumers of popular film, young children could take

Critical Peace Pedagogues—Shaping Teachers in Training **91**

a fun movie moment and transform it into deeply engaged dialogue about complicated ideological frameworks. Role play activities, spontaneous writing and further open ended discussions about *Zootopia* could have the potential to spark ideas about school wide peace curriculum. Alongside adopting films that are popular in the media, parsing political speeches and rhetoric can also become unofficial lessons. Following up on the question of fear, oppression and peace, students were asked to analyze the Disney film *Zootopia* to find similar themes that children could relate to. Through analysis of popular children's films, a discussion in class ensued about the type of lessons that could be developed related to peace education. Below are several examples of a thoughtful analysis from pre-service educators related to the film *Zootopia*. Through analysis, my students were able to bridge the film back to the classroom.

> This movie reminds me of what is happening in the United States of America with the Black community. This was a big thing over the summer and last year. African Americans all over the nation were being shot and killed for no apparent reason. They were being stereotyped. It all started with the Trayvon Martin case and it just went viral after that. Police officers feared the black community. So instead of giving them a chance to surrender and go through a fair trial like every other American citizen they murdered many African American men. Trayvon Martin had a hood on and was walking in the night and George Zimmerman shot him and eventually killed him based on stereotyping of a black male. In this society African American males are seen ad drug dealers, gangsters, and people who steal. When in fact everyone steals and everyone gangbangs. Society had placed these bad profiling ideas on the African American community. This forces others to be afraid and therefore violate the human rights of them. In my opinion the movie will give the new generation a great idea of profiling and social injustice. It displays the real world problems in such a great way of understanding for kids.
>
> *Zootopia* is a film that mentioned a lot about marginalization; in this case it was of predators. The predators are prejudiced as a whole due to the 14 predators that had gone 'savage'. This parallels to how Muslims in the United States are being prejudiced as a whole due to terrorist attacks by extremist Muslim groups like Al Qaeda and ISIS. Groups like this are targeted for marginalization, and after attacks like 9/11 and the more recent attacks in Paris, the government and media have installed more and more fear in the people. Nick the fox can represent an innocent Muslim citizen of the United States, and the bunnies can represent the percentage of the American population that stereotype all Muslims as terrorists. Judy the rabbit can represent those people who, despite not stereotyping all Muslims still carries that fear that has been spread onto the population. This is shown by the fact that she always carries the fox repellent with her and at two points in the movie

92 Critical Peace Pedagogues—Shaping Teachers in Training

prepares herself to use it, once when she first sees Nick and stereotypes him involuntarily and again when she becomes frightened by Nick after the news of the 'savage' animals is released and she gives a press conference that furthers the fear of predators. Nick's story from his childhood is an example of the many cases we have heard of Muslims, or even people who look like Muslims to the ignorant eye, being stereotyped and harassed simply for where they come from or what they look like; their 'biology'.

In many ways, this film directly correlates modern day America. Our society has categorized every individual into boxes based on their physical appearance, which consequently prevents them from breaking free into something beyond the exterior. *Zootopia* conveys a common theme that concerned two groups of species: the oppressed (prey) and the oppressor (predator). In the United States, there are distinguishable oppressors and oppressed individuals. Donald Trump is a perfect example of an oppressor in modern day society. Some may say that his opinions on minorities bring out the subconscious thoughts of many. Numerous Trump supporters have been offenders of oppression recently. Racism and prejudice are more evident than ever since the 1960s. Trump is bringing out the worst in people and he is actively encouraging acts of hatred and supremacy. He is empowering racial oppression and prejudice to 'Make America Great Again'. Oppressors believe his statements and use this to validate their acts of oppression towards the oppressed. These instances have only caused a greater divide between the two group, which pushes us further away from progress in eliminating prejudice.

The Disney film *Zootopia* provides a telling example of how government and state authority can be used to undermine the rights of people and compromise their image. Despite being a children's film, it contains a very deep message that can be seen to have many parallels in the world. Far too often, the will of bigoted and racist government figures can be carried out in the form of violence and mass prejudice against a set of people. Upon watching the film, the first thing that comes to mind is the troubling parallel that can be observed between *Zootopia* and the Holocaust. Adolf Hitler had a deep hatred of the Jewish people. He longed for a way to exterminate those he hated and provide a route for the formation of a pure German race. Similar to the Assistant Mayor in *Zootopia*, he used the power of his position to spread his hatred for certain people throughout society. This type of sentiment among a population is dangerous because it fuels hatred and teaches young people of a society that marginalization and prejudice against certain people is the accepted norm. Similar to the predators who were being targeted and manipulated by the state, the Jewish people who resided over any land that came under the jurisdiction of Hitler were tracked down and targeted. Indeed, it is truly astounding to think of the horrors that can be brought against a people when they are being targeted by none other than the government itself and therefore have no viable method of defending themselves against violent targeting. In my opinion, there should be robust and thorough examinations of all elected officials and their endeavors throughout the world. Government as we know it is intended to serve the people, not persecute the people. Therefore, if state authority finds its way into the hands of a racist or bigot, there can be dire consequences for those who are the subject of that person's hate.

Hate and its ensuing violence are rarely addressed in the classroom. There are, however, strategies to bring this conversation in to the classroom. Concurrently while taking teacher-training courses, many students are engaged in their student teaching practices in the classroom. From time to time, students enact spontaneous lessons related to hate, peace and social justice and I will share one brief example.

A Bag of Peanuts and Mr. L. Beginning the Journey as a Teacher Activist

Bringing class discussions to life around global crises as they are taking place requires great skill, insight and facilitation skills. Bringing in "current events" is merely the first step in shaping global citizens. Allowing students to critically engage in topics can allow for a much more meaningful engagement. A student of mine, who I will call Mr. L., was simultaneously working in the Harlem Izone schools and taking a methods course shared valuable stories of their critical and transformative work. Allowing students to analyze political rhetoric and commentary can open uncomfortable discussions and dialogue. Although controversies are revealed, Mr. L. used the words of Mike Huckabee to have a powerful discussion on human dignity in their 7th grade class. Mike Huckabee paired his aggressive call for military action in the Middle East with a vocal rejection of Syrian refugees fleeing violence in their home country. He compared the hundreds of thousands of displaced Syrians to "peanuts", further saying that we can't risk bringing terrorists into the country along with refugees.

> "If you bought a 5-pound bag of peanuts and there were about 10 peanuts that were deadly poisonous, would you feed them to your kids?" he said. "The answer is no".
>
> Mike Huckabee November 17, 2015 MSNBC

Students were asked to respond to Huckabee's comment and his inciteful stance on refugees. Students were first allowed to respond with their thoughts.

> Peanuts? How can you talk about peanuts?
> Humans are not peanuts! That is just horrible—humans are not objects— they are living beings.

> Huckabee is being irresponsible by calling people a food item. He takes away their dignity.
>
> Politicians could be calling any group of people they don't like as unwanted poisonous peanuts.
>
> Didn't people in Rwanda call the Tutsis cockroaches they told people to weed them out? If you call Syrians peanuts—that's the same thing.

Mr. L. followed up with these comments and added the idea of human dignity to the conversation. What would it look like if we were treat Syrian refugees with dignity? How can political language that takes away their dignity be responded to? The teacher had a very powerful discussion with his students about the dehumanization of refugees and the need to be critical consumers of the news and the stances of politicians. Students then were asked to replace the phrase "bag of peanuts" and brainstorm dignifying phrases. Students were keen to focus on the plight of the refugees and noted that naming them as "migrants" as the media repeatedly had, also minimized their displacement and the violence they faced.

Mr. L. also engaged his students in a careful analysis of the Universal Declaration of Human Rights in their classroom. Mr. L. enacted his lesson in our course. Key highlights in his lesson were the spontaneous manner he would take the topic and continually develop his goal as students tackled the topic. The lesson began with a serious discussion about rights versus responsibilities and ended with a rewriting of articles outlined in the universal declaration. For example, more clarity was rewritten into Article 16 on the Right to Marriage and Family. The original article reads: *Men and women of full age, without any limitation due to race, nationality or religion, have the right to marry and to found a family. They are entitled to equal rights as to marriage, during marriage and at its dissolution.* Students with full understanding of LGBT rights wished to include a clause that marriage would be considered between individuals regardless of sexual orientation. Students then had a conversation about DOMA or the Defense of Marriage Act and the current measures to undo gains for marriage equality. Mr. L. teaches in a predominately low income minority community, yet is immersed in lessons with digital citizenship. Current events are relevant to his students' lives such as the Black Lives Matter movement and police brutality. As a white male who had grown up in suburban New York, he spoke about his positioning as an outsider and how his convictions about great teaching allow him to use his classroom space to be a deeply creative and transformative place for his students. His position of privilege was not a barrier to his convictions about teaching transformatively and he understood that there would be a majority of students who would understand the exposure to oppression as a mere classroom exercise. There were a few students, however, who took the powerful lessons to become true agents of change and activists. Students in Mr. L.'s class were motivated by classroom discussions to participate in marches related to Black Lives Matter and developed an awareness campaign in their school about police brutality and an awareness of their rights when faced with an encounter with law enforcement. Local area law enforcement agencies also participated in the awareness campaign.

In my previous book, *Be the Change: Teacher, Activist, Global Citizen*, the work of my former teacher education students was highlighted to elucidate the possibilities for peace praxis. The sustained impact of our classroom dialogues was further developed within their own classrooms as novice teachers and provided some evidence of where possibilities are positioned for critical peace pedagogy. This "multiplier effect" that is spoken about in peace education circles can be realized. In the book, attention was also drawn to the intersection of global citizenship, peace and classroom practice through numerous global examples with topics ranging from the Israeli-Palestinian conflict, Rwandan genocide victims and survivors of the Khmer Rouge killing fields to local farmworkers labor rights. Within these various contexts, teachers and students alike became activists participating in peace activism and global citizenship. In order to cross borders and allow teachers from various global sites to engage in a productive dialogue, I organized an international conference on teaching peace and human rights.

Connecting Teachers Globally

We come to you today from our country, Kenya, we are the Masai. We are a nomadic people and our rights are violated every day by our government. We come to you as teachers, to share our plight. Students in our classrooms must walk long distances, our schools have few resources and we need to make the world aware of our struggle. People like to watch our tribe dance and the Masai are known for our red robes, tall people, jewelry and jumping dances—but we are a people that are used by Kenya to be the attraction for tourism and business. We are exotic—and that lures you to come to our land and spend your money. Kenya should take care of us. We are not puppets—we are everyday people who want education, medical care and proper rights.

(Masai tribal members UN Annual Teach for Peace
and Human Rights Conference)

Masai tribal members, teachers from India and Mexico along with teachers from around the country gathered together for a United Nations conference on Teaching Peace and Human Rights. The idea of a global consortium of teachers engaging and sharing ideas across international borders became the basis for an annual conference I directed in conjunction with the United Nations. The goals of this conference were twofold. First, teachers were brought together to take various workshops run by local NGOS and human rights organizations. Workshops and presentations spanned the spectrum of

96 Critical Peace Pedagogues—Shaping Teachers in Training

human rights issues. The Masai tribesmen have secured a place within the lives of those that attended the conference-multiple teachers have in fact visited them in Kenya to continue the dialogue about their rights and cause. Throughout the conference, teachers were provided with strategies and curriculum ideas to take back to their classrooms. Second, teachers were to engage across international borders through videoconferencing at the UN headquarters in New York City to exchange ideas, dialogues and innovations about peace education. Teachers came to hear the stories of one another through videoconference from countries such as Mexico, Tanzania, Kenya, The Philippines, Pakistan and India. At the United Nations, teachers developed a mutual international plan of action on the incorporation of human rights pedagogy in the classroom. This Plan of Action was in support of UNESCO's International Decade for a Culture of Peace and Non-Violence for the Children of the World campaign (2001–2010). For seven consecutive years, this conference served as a powerful platform for the exchange of ideas and fostered possibilities for meaningful global citizenship. Stemming from knowledge gained at the yearly conferences many local area teacher activists went on to create their own organizations. The conference served as a catalyst for many activists. As a platform to engage and seek ways to forge a politics of interruption, the seeds were planted for long term initiatives in peace activism and global citizenship. J. Jill Rito, a local area teacher, believed the Teaching for Peace conference served as a platform for her impactful initiative on dialogue across borders to combat Islamophobia and nurture dialogue and understanding among youth of different cultures and religious traditions.

Dialogues Across Global Borders

> Finding the commonalities despite the obvious differences came through sharing, listening, learning, understanding each other or at least trying. That same openness towards acceptance became a valuable asset in the teaching profession. And although language in communication is important for me as a foreign language teacher, the culture and content are equally as significant in my quest in reaching others, forging human relationships and being an active part in the lives of others.

The work of teacher activist J. Jill Rito illuminates transformative and radical work that is deeply meaningful and occupies the counterhegemonic space. As an Italian language educator, Ms. Rito was able to develop unofficial curriculum frameworks through extracurricular activities that were deeply committed to global citizenship and peace activism, albeit within a lens of interruption about Islamophobic forms. As political events unfolded globally after 9/11,

J. Jill Rito felt compelled to resist the racist nativism and Islamophobic rhetoric that was so prevalent.

> In 2001 after the events of 911 unfolded, a deepening suspicion and darkness seemed to creep into the lives of many American students with foreign family origins. To show unity, we formed a group called **Students United** and began to address the emotions, the words, actions, confusion taking place. One day in an Italian language class, the idea arose of expressing the same emotions with different words. Students thought of words like peace, unity, strength, courage and thought of them in their learned language and their families' language at home. Soon, we had scraps of cloth on which words from 15 different languages were sewn into a quilt of solidarity. That quilt was received by Commissioner Ray Kelly of the NYPD at 1 Police Plaza with Matilda Cuomo and our students. It was placed in their museum then. There are many more experiences which come to mind, but the lesson learned is that when we have and develop empathy for others, we find ourselves.

These initial moments of solidarity became the planted seeds of a greater project to connect directly with youth in Afghanistan.

J. Jill Rito described the program with the Afghan Peace Volunteers:

> The Afghan Peace Volunteers are a group of young men and women who each month on the 21st, (and also by special arrangement outside of the 21st) connect with students, professors, teachers and other interested parties via Skype or Livestream in what is known as a Global Day of Listening. The group is led by Dr. "Hakim" (MD—Dr. Wee Teck Young) from Singapore who, when working in an Afghan refugee camp, listened to the voices of the war-weary youth seeking to live a life of non-violence in the midst of indescribable misery. From our beginnings in speaking with them in 2010, they have grown to build a school in Kabul, teach English, help clothe, feed, educate street children and teach non-violence through the philosophies of Gandhi and Dr. Martin Luther King, Jr., make and distribute duvets free of charge for the frigid Afghan winters and teach many women to become seamstresses and earn a livelihood through growing independence and self-reliance. Their courage and tenacity are nothing short of amazing. At first my students were shy and embarrassed about asking questions. Things like, "What's your favorite food?" and "What do you do on weekends?" served to emphasize the culture divide, lack of basic knowledge and the awkwardness of initiating contact. As connection times became more frequent, the APV would greet students by name, they would remember who spoke to them the

98   Critical Peace Pedagogues—Shaping Teachers in Training

month before and anyone could feel the barriers of language and cultural diversity melt as friendships took hold.

One memorable question came from a young man Ali, who innocently asked one group of students, '*What can we do to make you stop hating us?*' I think that for a brief instant, all the news broadcasts about the savagery of the Afghan people slammed into a profound, new reality for me and for others. There was no blame in his voice, no divisiveness, no anger, hatred or violence. He wanted to find the catalyst in himself to change and arrive at peaceful terms between lands, among people. This from someone who had nothing but the spirit of hope and desire left me stunned.

This moment that J. Jill Rito describes is powerful. In many ways this moment is where the meaning of "peace" is recast; it calls for a negotiation in ideology for the American students as waging "violent war" has been the means to achieve "peace". Assumptions about privilege and power are disrupted and this confrontation is where uncomfortable dialogue can lead to possibilities of reconciliation. When asked how Afghan Peace Volunteers symbolize global citizenship and critical peace activism, J. Jill Rito shared the following:

By extending a reach across borders, cultural and language confines as we have done with the Afghan Peace Volunteers, we facilitate a basic human understanding and awareness that thrives on an existential level. This reach of global community and citizenship holds mystery, spirituality and depth which when nurtured and encouraged to grow, brings the potential for change and progress among people. These, to me, seem to be the seeds of admitting that, despite the reluctance to say the word, 'PEACE' unless in a ritual of worship, everyone, everywhere wants to live in peace. Peace is the desire of all mothers for their children, their husbands, their families, nuclear and extended. It is the spiritual cement of progress, triumph, development and well-being. It is a proud and honorable goal which contrary to the opinion of many exemplifies true strength rather than weakness.

In further reflection about her work, J. Jill Rito encouraged other teacher activists to begin and continue their work.

Most people who are involved in peace and justice issues are motivated by a deep desire to make life meaningful and better for the many who for whatever reason cannot or are limited. They are more than eager to share their stories, their resources and expand for the benefit of furthering the causes. Reach out to all the resources that exist, personal and professional. Follow your heart and spirit. Work with passion and persevere. There are ways to weave these realities into curriculum and there are plenty of people waiting to assist in implementing a plan. Just ask.

Unofficial curriculum and initiatives such as those by J. Jill Rito bring to life the ideas that have been set forth so far, Global Days of Listening provides youth with a counter-narrative to the stereotypes and Islamophobic sentiment-and for youth to have an opportunity to dialogue. The human connection and video conference interaction creates openings where youth are invited to understand that all voices matter.

A Pig in a Poke

I would like to end this chapter with a personal story that illustrates well some of the tensions that can arise through scholar and teacher activist work. Years ago, as a young graduate student, I applied to participate in Harvard University's World Teach program. I selected Namibia for my site placement. The program haphazardly placed us in a rural town with very little background preparation or understanding of what to expect. Our task was to fulfill the role of teachers (that are deeply lacking there) and to incorporate technology into the classroom to narrow the digital divide. Now, putting aside romantic notions of "saving" children in Africa, the experience came with some very real lessons about our role in this small village. The work we were doing was important and as volunteer educators we took the task at hand seriously. In theory, the idea of the Namibian National Ministry of Education hosting volunteers to teach in their schools to fulfill the needs of their students bears all the assemblages of a workable program. What were our intentions? How were we received? Were we viewed as outsiders?

From the perspective of volunteers we were placed in harm's way—several female volunteers along with their peace corps counterparts were held up by machete point, in their dormitories and were assaulted and robbed. This experience was very raw and provoked a windstorm of personal introspection about the meaning of peace activism. In the book, *That the World May Know: Bearing Witness to Atrocity*, James Dawes (2007) speaks about the emotional toll that peace work can take upon volunteers and aid workers. These moments of vulnerability, fear and rejection are real. There is anger—that one can begin with the most honest intentions—yet putting oneself in harm's way does not have to be the means to achieve the ends.

I felt compelled to put my experience down on paper and submit my work to an academic journal. Sharing the experience was important for me and in particular, deconstructing the role I played as a teacher activist in the World Teach program. I also spent quite some time analyzing the contradictory spaces where volunteers were poorly prepared to teach. It was when I received reviewer comments, I was reminded that activist work can be quickly diminished and delegitimized. The reviewer comments went as follows … "the paper fails to contribute theoretical knowledge and quite frankly, the author's story sounds like they bought a pig in a poke".

I found this comment to be deeply disrespectful and offensive—but it reminds me that not all activist' work is viewed as legitimate. The reviewer insinuates with the comment that activist work ought to be compartmentalized and controlled–that experiences can be sterilized and void of the unexpected. To buy a pig in a poke requires that I as the consumer was foolish to engage in the experience without full understanding of its contents—or quite simply to assume activist work in the rural developing world be devoid of crime would be ignorant. Or for that matter, it required me to understand my place of privilege. I never published that work in respect for my fellow volunteers, as their experience did not deserve revictimization or for that matter theoretical elegance. The question in my mind nevertheless continued to remain: How can we as teachers actively work to achieve peace activism despite wearing multiple identity hats, albeit one may be of privilege? The journey of one activist teacher will bring this question to life in the next chapter. Through an autobiographical narrative spanning multiple decades, one teacher activist invites the reader to understand the challenges, setbacks and victories that can be faced when teaching peace behind closed doors in the face of great adversity and a political climate that purports war.

6

INCREASE THE PEACE

A Journey of a Teacher Activist

The journey of a teacher activist is nevertheless a story of struggle and setbacks. Given the tremendous resistance that one may face when embarking on topics of peace, human rights or even to question the culture of a school and community, it requires an intrinsic commitment. Curriculum that departs from the norm is often deemed "controversial" or a deviation from the responsibilities of a teacher. How do teachers answer back in times of crisis? The challenges that I faced as a secondary school teacher shortly after 9/11 were illuminated in my article in *Radical Teacher* in 2005. In the article, I wrote about the incorporation of 9/11 into my world language course and the difficulties in finding the spaces in which to develop the conversations around the topic. Teaching about 9/11 was considered "unpatriotic" yet the movement to interrupt Islamophobic sentiment was beginning to take shape as coalitions across the country worked to undo and disrupt racist nativist forms. The experience of resistance to "controversy" has also been well argued in the work of Diana Hess (2009). Diana Hess poignantly builds her arguments about the necessity of democratic participation and challenges the reader to think about the defining frameworks that are laid out in regard to what "good" citizens in a democracy are supposed to do. Of course, prescribed curriculums and strict agendas attempt to define for teachers and students what knowledge is of most worth—hence forming the a core set of knowledge for "good citizens" to participate in society. This core knowledge requires ongoing disruption.

The following chapter will highlight the journey of a teacher activist, from the beginnings in his English classroom, to building a grassroots social movement around human rights to life-long contributions to the LGBT community. This teacher activist has positioned himself in unique ways to become accessible to student inquiry and explorations about the difficult questions. This case study illustrates well how powerful conversations and ideological confrontation

102 Increase the Peace

can take place in unofficial curriculums that further develop into localized student run peace activist movements. Transformation in the classroom takes place when the educator possesses the identity of a teacher activist. As a teacher activist in a classroom with learner activists, powerful dialogues and actions can take place for conscientization, humanization and transformation. The journey of a teacher activist is oftentimes illuminated by setbacks and challenges and these experiences can embolden teachers to continue forth and develop greater initiatives.

Increase the Peace

> In all my years as an activist, it comes back to respect. Respect is where it begins and ends in order to interrupt racist, sexist and homophobic ideas. No trust leads to no respect of others.
>
> Bruce Castellano

The 1970s were an era when multiple movements were gaining momentum. Movements around racial politics, women's rights, the feminist movement and the gay rights movements as well the anti-Vietnam war movement were gaining traction. It was during this time that students in the classroom were deeply engaged in these conversations and concurrently working through their own fears of the military draft. During these tumultuous times, marginalized groups continued to fight for equality and protest the war. Simultaneously, a "New Right" movement was also taking hold and mobilized in defense of political conservatism and traditional family values. To teach during this era meant navigating a landscape where social experiments, struggle and economic uncertainty permeated the lives of students and teachers alike. The journey of one teacher activist from this era through to contemporary times illustrates well the multiple strategies of resistance that can be employed in the unofficial counter-hegemonic curricular space.

The year was 1971 and in the midst of these political and social battles, Bruce Castellano was hired as an English high school teacher in a blue collar working and middle class community in suburban Long Island. He describes the community as then having a student community that for the most part had provincial views and described themselves as closed off of the rest of world and not trusting others. At the same time students were eager to reach out to their changing world. Bruce described the climate during his early tenure as a teacher.

> The country was split about the war, in the classroom students were being drafted and as a teacher close to their age I had not been drafted and it inspired me to connect differences. Teaching controversial issues was easily connected to the social movements around us and many students wanted to get involved and be politically engaged.

It was not simple, however, I had to adjust my teaching approach to the community. As a teacher, you would experience fellow teachers who were openly making derogatory comments to students. Teachers would say things to students faces—racist, sexist, derogatory—girls were put on the spot—jokes were greatly offensive—under the guise of we are all white, straight and Christian here. While there was a significant part of the staff who was accepting and eager to initiate social change—some of them felt powerless to do so.

The teaching climate that Mr. Castellano describes resonates with the challenges of the political climate where leftist movements were facing the "New Right" movement. In his early years, Mr. Castellano had to develop unofficial strategies to address the needs of those students in the classroom that hoped to be politically engaged.

Mr. Castellano noted the following,

I had to engage in a modified approach to controversial issues pre tenure, and I was labeled a hippie. Students would label me as 'gay but not out'. In an environment where you could lose your job and be a pariah, I treaded on the don't ask, don't tell bubble. This however diminished towards the end of my career in the late 1990s.

Mr. Castellano understood that his teaching was constrained as he was obligated to adhere to strict curriculum guidelines.

As an English teacher I was dealing with curriculum guidelines that were about all the classics or the 'dead white men' curriculum. The stuff was based on Eurocentric celebration and was the traditional approach to English. The curriculum was 'safe' and it was not until the early 90s that we brought in work by women and people of color—and because the curriculum was so jam packed with time constraints—we could not bring in more larger works by alternative authors. I began to incorporate an unofficial curriculum on controversial issues slowly. I initially brought in war songs and lyrics and used unofficial lesson plans. I brought in short pieces related to what we were reading such as articles, short stories, poems, song lyrics or even a vignette from a play.

Mr. Castellano speaks about the social climate of his students during these times.

What struck me was a 'bubble' mentality and I was really upset by how students were 'socially' back in the 70s and 80s—I felt they were immature when it came to the world—they would complain about wanting to get off the island, but feeling fearful to do so, feeling constrained—so I would plan these field trips and would take students to Brooklyn and New York City. The students, of course made assumptions about the city—that it was a big bad place. But they were willing to explore new terrain and ideas.

Mr. Castellano further noted that students' association with the rest of world as unsafe stemmed from their lack of cultural awareness and even perhaps their absorption of what was being heard and said in the news and politics. He was inspired to bring them to different places in their lives. Sharing an example of guest speakers also illustrates student responses as limiting. He described the fact that bringing in guest speakers was like walking on thin ice. It was a cause for alarm as it was deviating from the curriculum. One guest speaker, one of The Beats, wrote Beat literature and was subversive and came in as a guest speaker to talk about poetry and the kids were laughing and making faces. He understood that as a subversive guest speaker coming into an ultraconservative group of students the theme of being your own person and writing from your heart further to see the world through other people's eyes was a concept that they were not familiar with.

Mr. Castellano described these examples as "tip toeing through the culture of the school in the beginning" and he did not feel comfortable with the restraints and felt that he needed to do things internally in the classroom. He described an early example of where teachers were allowed ownership of unique curriculum. These were short 10 week courses that students were allowed to take. Several teachers embraced this new curriculum. Bruce developed a course called Contemporary Music and Lyrics. In this course, students conducted music reviews, went to concerts and did biographies. He describes this mini course as being revolutionary because students were able to write about things that they were not allowed in the regular classroom—the overwhelming theme, however was related to sex, drugs and rock and roll. Mr. Castellano described some fellow teachers as being dismissive until he showed them what he was doing in class. They had to be convinced there was a real curriculum that was innovative. The way they were looking at the world was limited and prohibitive, unlike Mr. Castellano's activist lens.

Although he attempted to open up the mindsets of his students, he continued to view a naivete in their writing with no real connection between their lives and the people they idolized. As a teacher activist, the learners were not actors and not engaged to be activists. That lack of mutual space and synergy made many of the attempts at critical or counterhegemonic discourse by Mr. Castellano seem limiting.

Turning Point

Things then got serious. In 1985, the school was celebrating Black History Month and a commemorative poster of MLK was in the hallway. What happened next would set the trajectory for a student movement in the school led by

Mr. Castellano. The poster of MLK was defaced with a racist slur. This became a big issue in school—a school that had a small African American population. African American and white students approached teachers. It was Mr. Castellano who was the sole teacher who asked students to meet with him after school and talk about the incident. Mr. Castellano was only expecting four or five students to approach him after school, to his amazement over 30 students showed up and this inspired him to see a real cross section of the school that was represented. Anger, exposure and much venting about the racial and derogatory school climate characterized the initial session. Mr. Castellano thought to himself,

> What am I getting myself into because as I heard things that I was not aware of, and I thought: Where have I been for 15 years? Students were talking about things they hear every day from lots of people. There were everyday racist and homophobic jokes. Teachers would say things in the hallway as well as school aids. Students would say things to one another and teachers would not intervene.

After the initial meeting, students wanted to continue to meet. A storm had been unleashed. Mr. Castellano described the fact that he would come home more and more frustrated as he witnessed so much anger and venting yet nothing was being done. In meetings, students began arguing amongst themselves and would discuss what sort of things were okay to say, meanwhile it was obvious to him that none of it was okay. It was then that Mr. Castellano began to develop strategies. Students wanted to speak to other students in their classrooms. Mr. Castellano further stated that:

> This was dangerous because the students themselves had also been guilty of saying derogatory things, and they were not ready to mentor their peers.

Within his own school fellow teachers would ask him why he was doing this as an English teacher.

They would remind him that he was an English teacher and to teach his subject and that he was not a social worker. Or quite bluntly, he was told to, "Do your job". Over time, fellow teachers became supportive, and agreed for the need to have conversations about the school climate, but they themselves were not willing to jump on board. It was at this moment that Mr. Castellano needed to seek resources and research. One of the key findings for his students was the discovery of a local area consortium that disseminated knowledge on human rights and social justice. The consortium was just beginning to develop an educational outreach and he decided to take a group of students. In particular, a professional drama company that engaged in performances that were social justice and prejudice reduction based and these inspired his students and they wanted to take this back to the school. Students wanted to use the

106 Increase the Peace

role-play scenario framework to disrupt racist, sexist and homophobic slurs that were normalized in the school. Understanding how to interrupt it was challenging. The students then developed a pledge and a name for their work. They named their organization Increase the Peace and needed the pledge as a symbolic interruption.

Mr. Castellano reflected on the pledges that were developed.

The official pledge was written by ITP in 2003, as well as the elementary school pledge that was the basis for creating the high school pledge. The official ITP Pledge has evolved over the years. It was first created in a very simple form for elementary classes back in the early 90s. It started with the ITP students doing a lesson on the dangers and harm of hate words in grades 3, 4, 5 and 6 in the elementary schools. At the end of the lesson, students took the pledge, each got a printed copy of it and each classroom got a large poster sized pledge to hang in a prominent place. Teachers said that it was very effective and asked that we come in at the very beginning of the school year to set the tone for the year.

The HS ITP pledge was the idea of the students in the program, as most everything was. They said we needed a pledge on the high school level. It was created and written over the course of the school year 2002–2003. On April 20, 2003, the 4th anniversary of Columbine we had an unveiling of the pledge in mural size in the main lobby of the high school. It was an after school media event and local and national media attended. Newsday, Daily News, etc. We were interviewed by Ch 7 Eyewitness News and the pledge ceremony was taped and broadcast. I introduced the presentation and the senior members of ITP, (the captains and facilitators) took turns reading each of the nine pledge statements.

I learned that the pledge was taken down a couple of years ago and tossed in the trash by the administration to make room for an athletic display.

Several of my students also created a mural that swept across the entire wall of the cafeteria. It showed the words 'Increase the Peace' in 27 languages entwined with faces depicting peoples of various colors, faiths, ages, ethnicities, etc. It was some 30 plus feet long and 7 feet high and took one upper wall of the cafeteria. It was painted in panels and hung by our maintenance staff. I had excellent support from our staff.

Increase the Peace
Anti-Bias Pledge

All members of the High School Community, in order to ensure a safe, inclusive and caring environment for everyone, agree to:

- Respect one another
- Respect and learn from each other's differences and celebrate our similarities

- Recognize and appreciate the inherent value in everyone
- Think before speaking and always be aware that put downs and hate words are offensive
- Solve problems with discussion and never with violence
- Praise everyone's abilities; give support to anyone with disabilities
- Denounce all jokes and comments that are offensive to race, color, ethnicity, religion, gender, sexual orientation, age, appearance or disability because in the end they are more harmful than funny
- Accept and practice these beliefs and behaviors in our school, with our families, with our friends and throughout our community
- Always remember that peace begins with respect for all

INCREASE THE PEACE
The "No More Hate Words" Pledge
Elementary Students

I promise to never use mean or hateful words to ANYONE.

I promise to never say or do ANYTHING to make people feel bad.

I promise that if I hear SOMEONE ELSE use these horrible words, I will try my best to stop them from using them.

I promise that I will also HELP A PERSON FEEL BETTER, if another person says or does something hurtful to them.

Mr. Castellano describes his Increase the Peace program:

> Starting a Student-Based Human Rights/Peace Education Program. Every school should begin with the premise that the vast majority of students want to learn and grow in a safe environment. For every racist, sexist, homophobe and bully in any school, there are many more students who oppose the views of these individuals and want to do something to stop the hate. In addition, it is crucial that students learn that they are citizens of the world. A focus on local, national and international human rights issues will help promote this concept. Students should be the foundation for an Increase the Peace™ program.

The high schoolers then began to write scripts that would reenact real-life scenarios. Mr. Castellano remembers how it all came together when they did their first tour of middle schools. The most powerful development was that middle school students felt comfortable sharing very private and painful information about racism, sexism and homophobia. The decision to take the teacher out of the room when Increase the Peace was present was challenging—but when possible, led to more revelation and access to students' lives and experiences.

A trust began to be built with the Increase the Peace students. Younger children felt compelled to share their stories with them and ITP students

108 Increase the Peace

transformed themselves into change agents. ITP also counseled students who received discipline referrals concerning issues of prejudice and human rights offenses. The school administration deals with the punishment and passes the referral on to an ITP advisor. Students with such referrals are required to attend sessions with trained ITP members.

Mr. Castellano forged a space to allow them to be activists, mentors and social justice advocates. From the initial development, Mr. Castellano created an ITP elective course for 11th and 12th grade levels in high school, training students to create and conduct a district-wide ITP program. He also created the Human Rights elective for high school students that focuses on local, national and international human rights issues.

Castellano reflects on the development of the course.

> 2001 as a pilot elective and was made an official full semester elective for juniors and seniors in 2002. It was in the English Deptartment and was offered for full semester credit. I firmly believe that it was approved as a response to the Columbine shootings. I sold it to the BOE as a proactive measure to prevent school violence. If it had been at any other time it would not have been approved as a course by the BOE. That same year I created the Human Rights elective. Also a full semester for credit in the English Department. It focused on local, national and global HR issues. The ITP course was a hands on course that focused on class and assembly presentations. Students created presentations and workshops. I was able to take those students to schools. … at first in our own district and then to other schools in Nassau, Suffolk, Queens and Manhattan. I had taken students to schools for years when ITP was an after school activity, but now as a course it had power and teeth. The admin at the time was very supportive of students going out of the building on field trips despite the outcry that after 9/11, going into the city was 'dangerous'.

ITP not only worked to make real change in the local school environment, the organization was also successful in making a real impact with the creation of a task force. Along with three other high schools, ITP formed The Nassau County Anti-Bias Task Force in 1994. The task force grew to 14 schools across Nassau County. The task force met once a month to exchange activities, consult on events and information in each school. They also ran their own conference/forum, with guest speakers representing local, national and international human rights issues. The outlined goals of the task force were as follows:

Anti-Bias Task Force Goals

- To have students from various high schools meet as partners in peace, not solely as competitors, which is the standard forum for high schools to encounter each other.

Increase the Peace **109**

- To share concerns and problems regarding bias and violence among the eight schools in the task force.
- To share solutions and insights concerning acceptance of difference and peaceful coexistence among the various schools in the task force.
- To have each high school involved present workshops to the task force for the sake of practice and criticism, before each school takes those workshops "on the road" to other schools in the community.
- To learn from each other about the problems and concerns that high schools may have that are unique to that school, and to have other schools offer objective opinions and solutions.
- To invite outside speakers, facilitators and motivators to instruct and enlighten all members of the task force regarding issues of acceptance of difference and violence reduction.
- To create an atmosphere of peace and harmony which can serve as models for students to bring back to their own high schools.

Bruce Castellano continues to be an outspoken activist in the human rights community and in particular is working with national agendas on LGBT rights. In a recent talk given to university undergraduate students, Bruce focused on some of the key aspects of the history of LGBT rights and further on the outlook of critical peace and social activism. In particular, he provided students with powerful insight about the framing of the debate around the LGBT community. In class, Bruce asked the class to speak to him about the word "choice" and "sexual preference" in relation to the sexual orientation of individuals. Bruce provided a powerful answer to the students

> It is a political agenda to call it 'choice'. Human rights activists fight the word 'choice' and 'sexual preference' because choice implies the following—that if you chose this why should I protect your rights—you can choose to be straight. This also has fueled the mushrooming of 'conversion camps' for the LGBT community that is abusive and traumatic for the victim.

He also reminded students that history has been unkind to the LGBT community. The slow progress of being accepted, being granted rights and the backlash has hampered the overall human rights agenda. Bruce Castellano has lived through and has been an activist and advocate through the slow progress of the early 60s and 70s. Through the 1970s to the present he was an activist throughout the crashing blow to LGBT life and rights with the AIDS epidemic, to the scapegoating and victimizing of the community and into the current fight for marriage equality.

> When a group makes progress, there is backlash. And the backlash can be severe. During the onset of the AIDS epidemic, the gay community was victimized by the label of the "Gay Plague"—a pandemic was assigned to

110 Increase the Peace

one group. Gay men were dying of AIDs and there was no investment in AIDS research, it was only when straight individuals began to get to the disease that the bulk of AIDS research began. ACT UP became a new human rights movement at this time—it was an AIDS rights movement.

In the current political and cultural climate, Bruce Castellano illustrated to students how the LGBT community continues to face battles and setbacks for marriage equality and social and cultural acceptance. He notes that as a coping mechanism in everyday life the LGBT community continues to engage in acts of "covering" and this signals a setback. This, according to Kenji Yoshino, symbolizes an assault on our civil rights. Unlike assimilation, however, "covering" becomes a coping mechanism for fear of stigmatism and being profiled and targeted. In my previous work in Backlash: South Asian Immigrant Voices on the Margins, Sikh male youth abandoned the turban and Sikh cultural norms in order to avoid targeting and racist forms. This was an act that I described as "involuntary assimilation". Such enactments of "covering" can also be noted in many targeted groups that are racially profiled for example. Patriotic displays by Sikh and Muslim communities or the fear of adorning cultural symbols in fear of retaliation indicate these very real battles that are signal a compromise of civil rights in order to feel accepted and somewhat included into the fabric of daily life.

Kenji Yoshino further states that, "All civil rights groups feel the bit of the covering demand. African Americans are told to 'dress white' and abandon 'street talk'; Asian Americans are told to avoid seeming 'fresh off the boat'; women are told to 'play like men' at work and make their child-care responsibilities invisible; Jews are told not to be too Jewish; Muslims, especially after 9/11, are told to drop their veils and their Arabic; the disabled are told to hide paraphernalia they use to manage their disabilities. This is so despite the fact that American society has seemingly committed itself, after decades of struggle, to treat these groups as full equals" (p. 22). Yoshino believes that we are at a transitional moment in how Americans discriminate and further argues that this new form of discrimination targets minority cultures rather than minority persons and that outsiders are included-but only if we behave like insiders-only if we "cover". Using the frameworks of Yoshino's work, Bruce Castellano asserted the following:

> An LGB person is 'out' and still doesn't feel like they can be part of society. This individual doesn't want to lead a double life but may think in their minds that they may want that promotion, they want to get along with colleagues at work, they may be reluctant and choose not to hold their husbands hand in public for fear of being attacked. This is 'covering' and although it is a coping mechanism it is an assault on human rights.

Increase the Peace **111**

Playing along with hegemonic forms in order to participate in civil society and go unnoticed is symbolic of the treacherous landscape social activism can be. It also reminds us how difficult it can be to merely teach students to act up and speak up when they may consider their own safety and ability to function in society when doing so. Yoshino is serious about the dangerous cultural struggles for authenticity. He states "this covering demand is the civil rights issue of our time. It hurts not only our most vulnerable citizens but our most valuable commitments. For if we believe a commitment against racism is about equal respect for all races, we are not fulfilling that commitment if we protect only racial minorities who conform to historically white norms" (p. 23). Given these renewed battles, Bruce reminds the students that we must work tirelessly towards acceptance in the face of backlash.

In conclusion, Bruce asked the class about the future of critical peace activism and human rights advocacy given the seemingly difficult road that has been traveled for the realization of rights. One student responded that their most important lesson that they would take from this would be the importance of social activism. Students were reminded how human rights have also been appropriated and utilized in the agendas of those that are engaged in the backlash to the LGBT community, or more specifically in the name of "religious freedom and rights".

> Marriage equality is a symbolic win but is not leading to societal change. Religion has crossed into politics and the idea of 'doing good for my God' has galvanized the anti-gay movement. The religious Right is now at the forefront of blocking laws and the word 'choice' is being utilized to preach that LGBT is wrong. 'Hate states' are fighting marriage equality in the name of protecting their religious rights. In short, marriage equality is viewed as a threat or in violation of their human right to religion. Their rejection of marriage equality symbolizes their assertion of their rights.

Given the wins and losses for the LGBT movement, the focus of the movement is in constant transformation. The deadliest hate crime against the gay community occurred when forty-nine individuals in Orlando, Florida, who were in attendance at a gay nightclub, were killed in June 2016. This hate crime reiterates the brutality that the LGBT community faces in their daily lives. The crime was being described as a collision between terrorism and hate as resources assert that the assailant had pledged allegiance to ISIS (the terrorist network). In a statement by GLAAD,

> "Our hearts are broken for the victims and families of the horrific tragedy in Orlando", said GLAAD President & CEO Sarah Kate Ellis. "This unimaginable atrocity has not only robbed countless people of their loved

112 Increase the Peace

ones, it has also stolen a sense of safety within the LGBTQ community. As we mourn the victims of this unspeakable attack, we are also reminded that the work to end hate in all its forms must continue.

The Muslim Alliance for Sexual and Gender Diversity, which works to support and empower LGBTQ Muslims, declared in a statement released on Sunday,

> This tragedy cannot be neatly categorized as a fight between the LGBTQ community and the Muslim community. As LGBTQ Muslims, we know that there are many of us who are living at the intersections of LGBTQ identities and Islam. At moments like this, we are doubly affected.
> "We reject attempts to perpetuate hatred against our LGBTQ communities as well as our Muslim communities", the organization continued. "We ask all Americans to resist the forces of division and hatred, and to stand against homophobia as well as against Islamophobia and anti-Muslim bigotry".[1]

Homophobia, Islamophobia and targeting of groups work together to oppress communities, when victimized groups unite together an essential counter-voice is crafted.

The act is being understood as part of a reactionary homophobic movement and not an isolated incident. In conclusion, Bruce Castellano reminded students that social movements require allies and more often than not demand financial backing and the support of politicians. He stated that political clout was a key factor involved in making things move forward. As he described the historic bloody riots of Stonewall in Greenwich Village to present day battles, Bruce encouraged the students to become critical peace and global activists. He poignantly left students with the following advice,

> You are the generation of social media—use it wisely. Make a movement go viral. Use the loud voice of social media to be the voice for the silenced. I began my activism in my classroom and now I work with national campaigns and agendas with the LGBT community. You can start small. Activism starts everywhere and in small places.

This chapter has provided us with much needed insight on the journey of a critical peace educator in the classroom and beyond. Learner activists also play an important role as inspiring community activists and peace activists. Thus far, we have ventured into classroom spaces and have understood the moments of disruption that can occur when teachers make peace praxis relevant, yet what are the silenced stories of youth whose lives are embedded in violence who become community leaders? I would like to now share a story of triumph, courage and hope. The life of Soledad, a young Latina girl who grew up in the gang life reminds us that victims themselves can become beacons for advocacy and key partners for marginalized youth.

Notes

1 http://www.alternet.org/grayzone-project/mourning-and-solidarity-local-lgbtq-leaders-warn-against-islamophobia Sarah Lazare Alternet.

7

THE STORY OF SOLEDAD

From the Gang Life to Peace Activist

Our society has written off many youth in our schools and labels have been doled out; dropouts, gang related, not college track material. Injuries of race and class further become more oppressive with injuries of "nationhood" as undocumented individuals further become silenced and forgotten. Predominately Black and Latino youth have been excluded from national dialogue and projects around changing society. In fact, within the current political climate, these communities are being scapegoated with the blame for everything wrong in society. Solving the problems of these impoverished communities become commodified by "change agents" and their plight becomes a stepping stone for those individuals that choose to teach "them" in order to fulfill other pursuits; such as those in Teach for America programs. Students in teacher education are also provided a window to observe high needs districts in order to allow students to gain insight into the challenges they face, yet similar to curriculum such observations become spectator sports with little incentive to deeply care and desire to change the conditions around the lives of these students. We "commodify" their lives as we utilize their experiences in schools as "observation decks" for pre-service teachers. Alternatively in place of rejection these communities require committed and wholehearted acceptance. What shape does peace education take when we strive to transform gang-affiliated youth and to circumvent violence in their lives to something more hopeful? Similar to my experience in urban schools, the challenges in the lives of these students are daunting and require deeply committed teacher and community activists on multiple fronts.

What would it mean to empower youth within their struggles to take ownership of their lives and further become peace activists? Can students who have faced countless struggles and barriers to success in fact become successful? There are countless stories of transformation yet we miss the opportunities to

The Story of Soledad **115**

embrace them. The focus of this chapter highlights the struggles, journey and activism of one young woman who is young, Latina, undocumented and was a former gang member. Hers is a story of countless struggles to seek out a place of belonging and connect with teachers to care, to find a voice and to simply believe in an American dream. It is from the life story of Soledad that we illuminate the lived possibilities for *learner-actors* who become the community peace activist and voice for those that have been written off in society. Soledad found her path to an education, a career and activism through the support of community organizations and the individuals that took the time to make her life important. Soledad became victimized by structures of violence, both overt and covert. From her journey as a young child crossing the border from Mexico, experiences in the gang life to her marginalization in schools, Soledad spells out for us where countless opportunities were missed for schools and teachers alike to "see" and "hear" her.

As has been illuminated by countless examples in this book so far, a hallmark of peace education is to recognize violence in its many forms in the contexts of lived experiences and further to develop strategies to interrupt it in meaningful ways. It is more pressing than ever in the face of anti-immigrant rhetoric and campaigns to understand the intimate details of their lives. We owe individuals like Soledad our undivided attention in order to situate schools and educators to become allies to children in high-risk communities. As has been historically the case, we lose countless youth to senseless violence and given the larger societal attitudes and racist nativism, we become compliant with policies of exclusion and incarceration when we admonish opportunities to understand the life histories of undocumented children. It is with compassion, understanding and harnessing possibilities for the lives of at-risk youth that we may find small victories.

Only between 6–10 percent of gang related youth are female. Girls who join gangs experience school failure and have learning disabilities: *One out of three* girls in gangs have been in special education, lack involvement in positive activities in or out of school, face sexual abuse and victimization, family dysfunction, low income, engage in early drug use and sexual activity, and have emotional disorders and exposure to violence. They are regarded as "violent", "barbaric" and "disaffected". When the system has shut out these young women, and when everything around them sends them the message that they are not worthy, and are failures, how can unofficial curriculums, efforts at transformation and peace activism be of relevance to their lives? Visiting the words of Paulo Freire he reminds us of the following:

> For the oppressors, however, it is always the oppressed (whom they obviously never call "the oppressed" but—depending on whether they are fellow countrymen or not—"those people" or "the blind and envious masses" or "savages" or "natives" or "subversives") who are disaffected,

116 The Story of Soledad

who are "violent", "barbaric" "wicked", or "ferocious" when they react to the violence of the oppressors.

Yet it is—paradoxical though it may seem—precisely in the response of the oppressed to the violence of their oppressors that a gesture of love may be found. Consciously or unconsciously, the act of rebellion by the oppressed (an act which is always, or nearly always, as violent as the initial violence of the oppressors) can initiate love. Whereas the violence of the oppressors prevents the oppressed from being fully human, the response of the latter to this violence is grounded in the desire to pursue the right to be human. As the oppressors dehumanize others and violate their rights, they them-selves also become dehumanized. As the oppressed, fighting to be human, take away the oppressors power to dominate and suppress, they restore to the oppressors the humanity they had lost in the exercise of oppression.

(p. 54 *Pedagogy of the Oppressed*)

In many ways, when we speak of the oppressed speaking back to their oppressor, regaining their humanity and further restoring humanity to both, it is oftentimes understood as more of a symbolic gesture or motivational idea to engage in social activism. Rarely are we able to celebrate individuals, who from a position of absolute oppression become true champions of transformation and humanization. Marked by insurmountable injuries of race, class and gender, undocumented female gang affiliated youth become the forgotten and oftentimes dismissed population in public schools. Navigating the culture of punishment and an educational system that has abandoned them and written them off as a failure and to regain a sense of integrity and agency is critical. The search for a self-identity is a pivotal trigger in joining gangs. According to James Diego Vigil, "Acquiring a self identity in this group way fits in with other adolescent functions. The gang, has taken on the responsibility of doing what the family, school and other social agencies have failed to do-provide mechanism for age and sex development, establish norms of behavior, and define and structure outlets for friendship, human support, and the like" (p. 168). At–risk youth navigate dangerous landscapes of marginality, nationhood and belonging as well as fractured identities. The current anti-immigrant climate contributes to additional fears and setbacks for individuals who reside in the shadows of society. Policies around getting rid of these youth should be replaced by incentives to embrace them. Peaceful resolution needs to replace violent solutions.

Patchwork Gang Prevention Policies

Parveen Verma, representing an organization that worked with at-risk youth, walked the hallways of a local Midwest middle school when she was approached by a middle schooler who attempted to salute her with a gang shakeup. A gang shakeup is a signifying handshake of distinct gang affiliation. These markers are territorial, dangerous and potentially harmful when exhibited. As a former director of a gang prevention program, Parveen immediately pulled the student aside with great concern. She spoke to the students about the dangers of gang-affiliated signs and exhibits and warned them about loosely engaging in them. After speaking with the student, she went one step further to speak with the school leadership. Her concerns were met with a lackadaisical response. The school principal minimized her concerns and merely replied that students in the school were gang "wannabes", and that further these gang indicators were merely fun and games. According to Parveen, these were the very attitudes that failed to prevent or rescue youth from joining gangs. Such deliberate denial works in favor of the school district and their reputation, at the cost of "turning backs" on at-risk youth. According to a local area anti-gang task force, youth are being recruited at younger ages and the students she observed in the middle school were in every way potential recruits for local gangs. Social media, accessible to all age groups, has also become a medium for recruitment, displays or gang rivalry and the emergence of gang "raps" and musical genres.

Parveen reflected on the difficult work involved in gang prevention and further, the challenges involved in the rehabilitation of gang members who wish to leave the gang life. It becomes obvious that schools and teachers in many ways are the first lines of defense to recognize and prevent the proliferation of gang recruitment, affiliation and initiation. There is no place in the curriculum or the lesson plan for gang prevention and awareness. In opposition to that, the lack of concern or denial of their presence can do more harm to youth who are vulnerable. Community members and organizations have worked tirelessly in schools to work with at-risk youth. The "unofficial" work of these individuals has provided these youth with a counter message to society's labeling and criminalizing of their identities and bodies. The current political anti-immigrant climate and the rallying around walls and policies of exclusion demand a moment of pause to listen, hear and understand the voice and struggles of undocumented youth. The life story of Soledad, who I frame as a learner-activist provides the reader with a unique perspective on the tenacity of one young woman's activism and peace work. Her conviction about the ability of schools and educators to be key supporters and champions of peace is powerful.

"Saving Soledad"

Soledad is a native of Mexico. In Mexico her family was wealthy, well settled and she was well taken care of. There was no violence or connection to anything related to the gang life. She described a peaceful and productive life for her family. The draw to live the American Dream, however, brought Soledad and her family to an urban city in the Midwest. Her family initially traveled to America on a visitor's visa. This visa would expire after 6 months and the family remained in America. They were soon without status and became undocumented. Neither Soledad nor her family spoke English and school was

118 The Story of Soledad

a daunting place. Both of her parents needed to work to make ends meet. Soledad described her family as honest and hardworking. Their focus on "making it" in America made the hard work seem worthwhile.

It was unexpected for Soledad and her family to come face to face with the gang life. Her elder brother was the first to join the gang life. Soledad describes his experience as an unfortunate one. He was bullied in high school with little or no support from teachers and school staff. She described the schooling experience as follows:

> There were no support networks in place, and the gang promised protection and support. We were like shadows at school. Not seen and not heard and of course not understood. It was not a caring or supportive climate.

It was within a short matter of time that both of her brothers were fully entrenched in the gang life. Her brothers began to dress differently and Soledad was used as an excuse for her brothers to attend gang meetings and initiations.

> My brothers needed an excuse to get out of the house to go to gang meetings. My parents were not aware of their gang activity. They would take me along with them and say we were going out to play. It was a turning point in my young life.

Soledad, at the young age of 8, was exposed to violent and traumatic gang initiations. A gang initiation is a rite of passage that is created by each particular gang. Gang initiations can involve committing crimes, being violently beaten, sexual initiation and other forms of forced coercion. Soledad was exposed to drugs, alcohol, guns and weapons. Gang meetings would take place at the gang leaders' homes and her brothers would take her along. She was the only girl amongst the men. Soledad at times was asked to fight with other little kids as a form of preparation and future gang membership. Collectively, these experiences were traumatic and detrimental to her on many levels.

In recollection, Soledad remembered that she was immersed and taught the mentality of the gang.

> Somewhere and somehow during these moments, I lost my childhood. Little Soledad was no more. The little girl in me went somewhere deep down and far away into my soul. I learned to hide my feelings, my tears and my fear. I became numb to feelings and no longer felt like a human being. Where did my humanity go?

Many of the key rules of the gang life were no fear, no weakness, never wear certain colors, family, respect, show your worth and always have loyalty to the people in the gang who have your back. It was in the late 1990s that her brother

The Story of Soledad **119**

was killed by gang rivalry. The night her brother left to retaliate the rival gang he was arrested and deported. Soledad would also get deeply entrenched into the gang life. Soledad stated the following:

> In a way society pushed us into the gangs, we didn't speak English and there was so much racism. We came here and you are told about the American Dream. There is no dream, no American Dream. No one was there to mentor us or guide us. Society told us we were a lost cause. It made us grow up and believe we were a 'nobody' and up to no good. I thought I would end up the same way and be a drop out. There were no opportunities because we had no papers and we were led to believe that there was no hope.

As a young Latina woman in the gangs, Soledad survived in the shadows of society. She was on track to drop out of school and to continue in the dangerous lifestyle of the gangs.

Soledad described her downward spiral.

> I began to fear for my life. My life was constantly on the run—I was getting into trouble, and I worried about being shot dead. Sometimes I would think in my head that my mother would find me dead somewhere. My dead body would be thrown to the side like a piece of garbage. It would be the end of a life—a life that was never lived. I would cry in private. Nobody should see my tears—otherwise I would lose my strength as a gang member.

Soledad's life would take a positive turn towards hope and a better future. It was not until she began to visit a local organization for the Hispanic community, did she find a pathway out of the gang life and towards activism.

> Parveen met Soledad at the local community organization. Soledad was painting a beautiful mural and was using art as an expression of healing. She connected with members of the organization that became her voice and support.

Parveen remembered the first moment she met Soledad.

> A magnificent mural was going up in our organization. I was standing there and looking on with awe at the painting. And then this beautiful young girl turns towards me and says, 'Hi, I am Soledad'. Her turning towards me symbolized to me that she made that big step to embrace herself and a positive future. It will be a day that I will never forget.

Parveen encouraged Soledad to attend the Comunidad y Vida program that was geared towards gang-affiliated youth. The program was instrumental in

120 The Story of Soledad

turning around the lives of countless youth. When asked about the key moments or individuals that helped her out of the gang life, Soledad replied with the following:

> The local community organization gave me the opportunity to be someone, to be proud of something such as art and painting. It was a safe place and I did not have to worry about nobody—such as rival gang members or others that judged me. I felt welcomed and people wanted me to be there. I made connections and felt there was always someone to talk to. In many ways, they helped keep me alive and not get locked up. Everyone believed in me, no matter what my past and if I messed up, they did not give up one.

Schools failed her and her family. Soledad believes that poor school climate is where the downfall begins for many youth.

> Schools need more mentors and these should be people that genuinely care and want to help. We need positive role models and to know that someone outside of the family is there to encourage you to work hard. I believe if my brothers had a positive male figure 'mentor' in their lives to show them other things, my brothers wouldn't have turned to the gangs. There needs to be a sense of belonging within the schools and children should be taught to give back to the community and be given a sense of purpose and self worth.

One key area that Soledad was very serious about was the manner schools continue to miss opportunities and cues for at risk students.

> There is a big issue here in this community as most schools are in denial. They believe that there are no gangs here and that students are just 'wannabes'. But schools should realize that gangs provide protection and membership and identity similar to the ways schools have cliques like the jocks, geeks, popular kids, etc. Schools are not connected with their students. Only the good kids who represent the school like the athletes and academic students feel the connections in schools. They forget about the rest of us. We are overlooked and we are lost cause and we pretty much get ignored like ghosts walking in a school. There is so much ignorance.

Soledad also shared her ideas on what a good school model might look like that could provide the necessary frameworks to reach the entire student body.

> There should ideally be a mentorship program throughout the school year, for example a senior adopting a freshman in a mentorship relationship.

Schools need to give youth something that they can be proud of and to also hold them accountable to something to foster a sense of responsibility. I felt very successful when I was creating a mural in the local community organization. I felt very proud of my work and I felt successful.

In many regards, Soledad simultaneously became a learner-actor-activist as she was propelled into opportunities to be creative, to learn and to teach others. Through her own struggle to be heard, she became an advocate for her fellow gang-affiliated friends. Soledad credits her survival to the local community organization and consequently the teachers that became her strongest advocates. The violence of the gang life (see Figure 7.1) and the streets coupled with the covert systemic

FIGURE 7.1 The night they took you away, I was forced to grow up. You told me to go back inside. That everything was going to be okay … Our lives changed forever. I saw them handcuff you and take you away. Not one hug or a kiss. I regret not running after you, begging them to leave you. I was 6 years old the last time I saw you. I miss you bro RIP. Soledad.

122 The Story of Soledad

violence of schools shut out pathways to success and social mobility. The answer to violence was resistance to the frameworks that defined her as a failure. Her advocacy for at risk youth and insistence on peaceful school climates represent her ongoing journey as a critical peace activist in the local school settings. Soledad's former mentor, Parveen, continues her work with at risk youth and strives to find positive and peaceful pathways for these students. As a peace activist, Parveen is constantly aware of the forms of symbolic violence that oppress and touch students' lives and she demands recognition of those barriers and seeks openings to counteract them. Parveen shared the following story that illustrates the hidden barriers that her students face.

> Many of our high school students have been placed within government related internships in the local city area. In that capacity, our organization provided the students with official city employee ID bus passes. We were appalled when we came to know that bus drivers were confiscating students' ID passes and were told they could not ride the bus—essentially being accused that the ID passes could not possibly be valid—but rather stolen or counterfeited. This is another glaring example of the everyday forms of prejudice, profiling and racism that these youth face. Our work, however continues daily to be their greatest advocates.

There are countless examples where Parveen becomes the voice and advocate for her students. As a mentor and friend she extends herself to the community and cares deeply about their success. The unofficial work that Parveen engages in changes the lives of countless youth through presenting them with violent free alternatives and second chances. Her work is a political act that enables students to realize the possibilities of a counter narrative; one that requires opportunity and demands acceptance and the assertion that their lives matter.

Creating an Awareness About Gangs

> As you can see, in an effort to truly be effective and save America's youth and communities from the devastating effects of gang involvement we need to come up with innovative ideas that merge prevention and intervention strategies. It is vital to provide youth with alternatives to gang involvement if we want to be effective in reducing gang involvement and activity. I must emphasize the fact that it is easier to get a young person to never join a gang, than it is to leave a gang once they are already entrenched in the criminal lifestyle. Although intervention is extremely important to the success of any gang reduction program, more of our energy needs to be channeled on developing innovative gang reduction curriculums and activities aimed at educating youth in elementary schools. The days of extra home work help and sport programs are simply

The Story of Soledad **123**

not addressing the needs of these youth, and as a result it is vital that we adopt new tools focused on gang prevention.

Sergio Argueta

Based in the New York area, I have had the opportunity to bring the conversation about youth empowerment for gang affiliated youth into my college classrooms. Sergio Argueta, a social worker and peace activist, has visited my classes numerous times to speak to teachers in training about gangs in schools. He began his presentation with the following powerful assertion.

> I have been to hundreds of schools throughout the North East region, and no matter how hard the living conditions in that community might be, whenever a child is asked what they would like to be when they grow up, the answers are almost always synonymous. 'I want to be a lawyer … a doctor … an athlete … a nurse … a fireman … a police officer'. Some of these kids have the audacity to go as far and say, 'I want to be President of the United States of America someday'. The audacity of these young people to think they can achieve whatever they desire is something that leaves adults wishing they still had the ability to dream.

He went on to say the following,

> Regardless of their race, their socio-economic background, their religious background, or any other socially structured categorical framework we can place human beings under, these answers are always the same. I have never heard a child say I want to be a killer, a drug dealer, a murderer, a gang member. If this is the case, why are we losing so many children to gang involvement?

As a role model to youth from all backgrounds, Mr. Argueta has made his message, his life and his programs beacons of support and opportunity. His organization called S.T.R.O.N.G. has a vast outreach and impact. According to Mr. Argueta, his program serves many needs.

> S.T.R.O.N.G.'s sole purpose is to provide alternatives to gang life in an effort to save our youth. We are not 'anti-gang', we are anti-gang and youth violence. We are anti-drugs; we are anti-illegal activity that is destroying our community. We do not have anything against the gang involved youth, but seek to address the behavior in an effort to redirect young people. The concept aims to build a counter culture to gang life. In order to deter gang membership it is necessary to provide a positive peer groups to replace gangs. It is mandated that all youth involved in our program are identified as either gang involved or affiliated by school administrators, self-identification, law enforcement, or other source of

124 The Story of Soledad

referral, or be siblings of gang involved youth. Our goal is to provide them with an alternative to the street gang.

Further, Mr. Argueta stated that:

> This program focuses on discouraging gang involvement by helping to develop positive life skills and peer groups, as well as providing them with a forecast of what the future holds for them should they choose a negative lifestyle over a positive one. We currently have over 130 youth enrolled in our chapters, and many school districts are interested in implementing our program. As a result of our data collection, this program will be evidence based by the end of the year. This program has enabled us to further develop other initiatives and strategies aimed specifically at reducing gang involvement and violent gang/gun crime.

Similar to Soledad's work as a peace activist, Sergio Argueta has made national strides in his work to counter violence in the lives of countless youth. He is also a former gang member and has turned his lifework towards uplifting youth. With an intimate understanding of the challenges that youth may face and having disengaged from the gang life, Mr. Argueta continues to serve as a peace activist in the community despite the numerous challenges that exist.

> Guess what? The real specialists on gangs are not sitting at this table. The real gang specialists are still on those street corners. That particular kid standing on that corner has the ability to pull together 30, 40, 50 individuals and get them to go do drive-by shootings and convict crimes, for that particular gang has leadership ability. How do I know? That was me. Two years ago I lost two friends and felt I had nowhere to go. Now I have an associate's degree, I have a bachelor's degree, I have a master's degree. Now I'm a homeowner, I am the executive director of one of the leading gang-prevention agencies in this region.
>
> And I can honestly tell you, I mean, the question is where do you think I would have benefited my country or my part of the region most? Locked up in prison or actually doing what I do. I will tell you this if we have so many kids we've lost to this criminal justice system, if we have so many youth who are losing to the street plague, what are we doing? We need to ask ourselves: What are we doing?

Mr. Argueta leaves many to ponder further in regard to youth violence with his concluding statements about gang affiliated youth,

> Beyond the moving of lips, actions speak louder than words. People have the ability to put things down on paper when they have the resources.

But actions speak louder than words. The fact of the matter is our kids are not hearing this. Why? Because we're not acting the way we speak. S.T.R.O.N.G. developed a chapter and we're going to schools and we want to work with the most 'high-risk' population. We declared a war on poverty. That didn't work out too well. We declared a war on drugs. We have yet to win that war. Let's not declare a war on gangs. Instead, let us declare peace on our youth. After all, they are our children and they need us now more than ever.

Shaping peace activists on college campuses requires ongoing dialogue and exposure to radical ideas. Beyond teachers in training it is critical to engage students in all fields of study with critical peace education. In the final chapter, I will again invite the reader into my human rights seminar. The examples in this chapter only further help to elucidate the powerful dialogue that can take place when students begin to question what it means to be human, to have dignity and ultimately to have human rights.

8

INTERMITTENT INTERRUPTIONS

Patchwork Peace Narratives From a Human Rights Seminar

> Similar to Malala, as I was born my mother in particular was upset. She wanted two boys and a girl to make it 'even' somehow. My mother often jokes by saying that I should have been born a boy, that she really wanted one. Although she says it lightheartedly these types of comments are extremely sexist and unbecoming of a girl who is already born into a society where females are subtly seen as weaker and second rate.
>
> —Excerpt from Freshman student essay response to "What is your Malala moment?"

Throughout this book, the work of teacher and learner activists has been explored in the context of the K-12 educational setting. In addition to activism related to the lives of pre-service and in-service teachers, undergraduates preparing for various non-teaching related disciplines are critical allies as well in the realization of critical peace pedagogy. Unofficial curriculums on college campuses related to peace activism and global citizenship have traditionally been relegated to ad hoc lessons or the haphazard discussions that are encouraged through the agency of interested and activist faculty members. The development of peace studies, human rights and global justice programs come painstakingly slow and further once developed, they struggle to maintain an identity and long lasting support.

As is well argued by Ian Harris (1998):

> At the end of a century racked by violence and war, peace studies faces many problems in gaining broad acceptance by universities and colleges. On the positive side are the students, concerned about the violence in the postmodern world, who are idealistic and eager to learn about alternatives to violence. On the negative side are the university administrators who in a time of fiscal restraint are not able to support new disciplines, however

important they may be. Television news in the West daily gives the impression that domestic violence and street crime are urgent problems. The hesitance of faculty to embrace this new field also means that peace studies programs have a narrow base of support that is dwindling as the professors in this field grow older without more resources. In spite of the tremendous carnage of the twentieth century, the field of peace studies is in danger of remaining marginal in the next century. Further obstacles come from cultures that continually rely upon peace through strength strategies to provide security for frightened citizens who in turn have little knowledge of nonviolent alternatives. In response to rising levels of domestic crime, politicians are building prisons and hiring more police, rather than providing support for peace education efforts that could help prevent violence by teaching young people peace-making techniques

To begin college careers, universities embrace a common reading for incoming college freshmen in order to work towards common goals of shaping their students into global citizens and critical and active participants in a democracy. Select universities choose a particular Freshman Read that is required by the entire incoming student body, and this provides a key platform for faculty to develop lessons and discussions around proposed topics. For example in 2010, Inside Higher Ed reported that:

> Books about multiculturalism, immigration or racism were the most prevalent (60 colleges), followed by environmental issues (36 colleges), the Islamic world (27 colleges), New Age or spiritual books (25 colleges), and issues related to the Holocaust or genocide (25 colleges). Only 6 colleges assigned classics. The study also looked for other patterns in the selections, and reported that 46 of the choices have a film version, 29 are about Africa, 9 are related to Hurricane Katrina and 5 are about dysfunctional families. (https://www.insidehighered.com/news/2010/06/04/books)

The question of human rights can easily be connected to the annual selection of reading. Although freshmen begin their journeys with powerful discussions, the ongoing discourse wanes throughout their college careers. Social movements have historically gained momentum on college level campuses and the incorporation of global citizenship and peace activism is critical in curricular frameworks. The prevention of violence, or the ability to view alternatives to violence to resolve conflict are far removed from curriculum goals. At the university level, the concept of the human struggle, human rights and day to day violence both, overt and covert, seem irrelevant to students and their lives. Oftentimes, peace studies curriculums are largely theoretical, thus allowing students to merely engage with alternatives to violence from a disconnected lens. Making these issues relevant to the students is the first task at hand and further, how they choose to adopt and embrace peace activism, can be a hit

128 Intermittent Interruptions

or miss. The narratives shared in this chapter are drawn from a human rights seminar. Programs based on human rights and peace activism, although they provide powerful anchors to foster global citizenship and civic engagement, should ideally require an element of activism, hands on learning and foster a personal connection to the issues. Such disruptions and interruptions take on the nature of being unofficial curriculums, hence this chapter will be presented in that patchwork fashion. The development of the critical peace activist can be forged through dialogue and unofficial classroom engagements and further these lessons can resonate beyond the classroom walls as students embrace the politics of interruption as part of their greater journey.

The Gallery Walk

The classroom walls were covered with large blank poster paper and students were busily drawing images of the human body. I had instructed the class to use their artistic skills and through imagery draw "what it means to be human". Students wrote various comments around their hand drawn human beings. For example, students wrote:

> To be human is to have feelings.
> To be human is to have choices.
> To be human means you have a heart and a mind.

I asked them to add something further to their posters. What does it mean to have dignity? Students mingled and challenged one another on various definitions. Students defined dignity as honor, worthiness and even the right to live in freedom. These were very positive images that were presented by each student group. Each poster exuded a hopeful and peaceful interpretation. The class was then instructed to do a gallery walk. This gallery walk required them to visit one another's posters and admire the visual presentation of humans living in dignity. Students exhibited a positive and affirming energy during this part of the activity. I then proceeded to the next step in this lesson.

Each group was given a distinct identity for their artistic human being. With this given identity, students were asked to reinterpret their definitions if necessary. They were also instructed to think about their definitions about humanity, dignity and human rights through the eyes of this identity. I had provided the following identity labels: Syrian refugee, terrorist, murderer, child slave, sex worker, human trafficker and poor welfare mother. The tone of the classroom instantly changed as students struggled to develop the lens of their assigned identities.

As I walked around the classroom, students were frustrated. There was clearly a moment of disruption as the previous moment of positivity became troubled with controversy. A group of students was challenged to define the humanity of a terrorist. Questions were being asked about the dignity and humanity of a terrorist and whether or not they were entitled to human rights. As they struggled to develop a response, they began to address issues of torture, the right to a fair trial and even the right to an identity. There was thoughtful discussion about radicalization and the intention to understand why humans would choose terrorism. Similarly, the group that was working with the human trafficker label struggled to define the path of the human trafficker. Student posters suddenly transformed and became tapestries of conflict. The artistic portrayal of humans no longer held their positive qualities or interpretations. Students were then instructed to take a second gallery walk and engage in conversations with other groups about their posters. This gallery walk was characterized by intensity, scrutiny and silence. Questions continued to be asked about how a terrorist could possibly have dignity or human rights? Why are Syrian refugees being denied their rights? And further, are we all victims of human rights abuses and can we find a common ground of empathy for all? Students were clearly frustrated and at the same time enlightened to the complexities of defining human rights, humanity and dignity. When comparing the two gallery walks, the first being positive where rights were universal and the second walk where rights were clearly indefinable, students faced a disruption (see Figures 8.1 through 8.4).

FIGURE 8.1 With the above image titled, "I Am a Sex Worker" students reasserted that all humans deserve dignity and deserve to be equal.

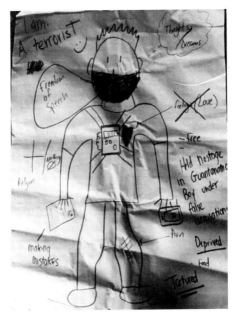

FIGURE 8.2 This particular group were given the task to define human rights for a terrorist. They succeeded in noting that torture and deprivation of basic needs was a violation of human rights and dignity.

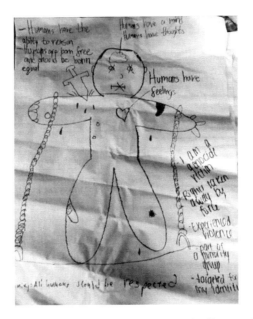

FIGURE 8.3 The image of a genocide victim was clearly illustrated with a denial of multiple rights such as being removed by force, targeted and experiencing violence.

Intermittent Interruptions **131**

FIGURE 8.4 The image of "I Am a Syrian Refugee" sparked emotional debate and the students clearly noted that these individuals were entitled to their natural born human rights.

This particular lesson resonated with students throughout the semester, as it posed the following question to them: Are human rights universal or political? It became critical as a class to constantly redefine the parameters of those that are stripped of dignity through dominant hegemonic forms and oppressive ideological frameworks. Understanding how social media strips dignity away from individuals in society also becomes an important lesson to develop with the class.

Media Consciousness and Stereotypes

Hurricane Katrina devastated countless lives, uprooted and displaced thousands and at the same time left little justice for those that were victimized by natures wrath. The first photo, taken by Dave Martin, an Associated Press photographer in New Orleans, shows a young black man wading through water that has risen to his chest. He is clutching a case of soda and pulling a floating bag. The caption provided by The Associated Press says he has just been "looting a grocery store". The second photo, also from New Orleans, was taken by Chris Graythen for Getty Images and distributed by Agence France-Presse. It shows a white couple up to their chests in the same murky water. The woman is holding some bags of food. This caption says they are shown "after finding bread and soda from a local grocery store".

Students were provided both images and are not given the byline. I asked my students to look at the images and develop a news headline for the images.

132 Intermittent Interruptions

Sample student responses have been:

Help! Survivors of Hurricane Katrina look for food as their lives are devastated.
Families seek to find food and supplies to take back to their families.
Knee-deep in devastation victims of Hurricane Katrina look for survival tactics.
Couple and young African American man seeking food and help during tragic events.

Students were then asked to look at the bylines that were originally used to describe the images. Students expressed disbelief and immediately questioned the situation and wondered if the reporter had in fact experienced the looting taking place. They were quick to realize that given the state of the community, looting, taking and finding can be loaded words. Coupled with the racial implications of the choice of words sends an immediate message to students about the power of the media and news to influence our perceptions about ideas. If Paolo Freire were in the room, he may perhaps remind us of the following, "Reading the world always precedes reading the word, and reading the word implies continually reading the world. As I suggested earlier, this movement from the world to the word and from the word to the world is always present; even the spoken word flows from our reading of the world" (Freire 1983 pp. 10–11).

After the initial discussion of the Katrina disaster byline students were asked to decipher the following sentences as well and determine how loaded words trigger vastly different reader reactions. What are the emotions that are conjured up through the choice of words? How is violence embedded in the different sentences? Does this violence further contribute to stereotypes and xenophobia? Can this be interrupted?

The class was divided into small groups and was given two sentences. Students were asked to close their eyes and envision what came into their minds when both sentences were read. The students' responses were very revealing about their own personal biases and assumptions about the world.

Group A:
The individuals began a riot. The individuals began a demonstration.

I envision a riot in a poor neighborhood, maybe lots of minorities that are upset about something. Maybe the riots in St. Louis or the burning down of businesses to protest something.

When I think of demonstration I think of quiet rallies—maybe the people in the Occupy Wall Street group. It's not violent.

Group B:

The woman was making a scene in the restaurant. The man was asserting oneself in the restaurant.

Some crazy blonde woman upset at her boyfriend maybe because he looked at another woman. Watch out it could get ugly!

The man is asserting himself over some issue with the order and it's quickly resolved because he is cool and collected.

Group C:

The extremists visited their place of worship. The devotees visited their place of worship.

Extremists make me think of Islam and Muslim worshippers—it might even be their allegiance to something shady.

Maybe it's like devotees going to the Vatican. Or maybe like Buddhists on a mountain side in Asia.

Much to their surprise, students reproduced racist, sexist and Islamophobic forms on the heels of a discussion about the discriminatory Hurricane Katrina byline. It was an eye-opening moment for students to realize that the extent of their participation in dominant hegemonic discourse had been rarely interrupted and they were easily perpetrators of forms of symbolic violence. This was hard to swallow for my students, yet it was a key reminder to them that the work of constantly being aware of how we read and know the world is complicated and requires constant interruption and analysis. In the lens of peace education, it calls for the need to constantly evaluate all forms of violence in order to build counter narratives.

The power that social media has to engage and mobilize youth is increasingly evident in social movements and idea making on college campuses. As consumers of media, college age students must also be included on the conversations about the hidden agendas of media that control our understandings about the world. Disrupting media messages that are loaded with oppressive meanings requires the incitement of awareness in students. The adoption of media consciousness in order to interrupt racist forms ideally should be learned in the formative years and is oftentimes never discussed until the college level, if at all. As I had shared with my chapter on teacher education, self-reflection is again central to dialogues about peace and global activism. At any given time frame, local, national or global events provide an opportunity to become critical consumers of the media. As critical readers of the world and word, alternatives to violence and oppression, this lesson became the basis of many classroom discussions throughout the semester. In particular, one incident comes to mind.

134 Intermittent Interruptions

Political Media and Oppression

> Honestly, I believe that Trump's policy and plan to temporarily ban Muslims right now is ideal because in the United States, we do not know who we are letting in to the country and they could be dangerous. I'm aware that most Muslims are great people, but the few that are awful create radical Islamic terrorism. Think about the gay nightclub massacre, the murderer claimed allegiance to ISIS and Trump reminded us that this is a reason to keep Muslims out.
>
> (student essay excerpt)

> Building a wall to prevent illegal people here from Mexico is such a good idea.
>
> It keeps out those that are not allowed here and then schools and teachers don't need to struggle with educating them. It also won't be an issue that they can't go to college—because they should only be here if they are legal.
>
> (student essay excerpt)

Complicated hegemonic forms are at work here. The emboldened nature of racial profiling and scapegoating of entire populations is wrapped up with an invigorated sense of gatekeeping and entitlement to "keep" America safe. Such rhetoric was strong after 9/11, yet the current climate has been noted to be more intense as hate crime watch groups and anti-defamation leagues from the Muslim and South Asian communities have reported. Stoking the flames of hate, with little opposing positive imagery of the Muslim and Sikh community, hate has also become an enterprise to mobilize and win elections. Patriarchal forms and racist nativism coupled with the increasing caudillismo by the presidential candidates has made it acceptable and even admirable for everyday citizens to act out and speak up. In many instances, an educator might draw away from such engagements with their students, knowing the murky waters that need be tread. It ideally should be, however, the great dialogue that an educator must have with their students in the journey towards transformation and dehumanization. In my previous work on the 9/11 backlash and research on teaching after 9/11 and the war on terrorism, I argued for the central role of teachers in unlearning hate and racist nativist forms, I continue to believe that and took every opportunity available to engage in dialogue and activities related to it.

Building on the dialogue and student commentary above, a student developed blindfold activity about racial profiling in my class again served to tackle the web of complicated knee jerk responses my students were expressing. Students were each given a distinct identity. Each student received a detailed profile about his or her gender, race, class, sexual orientation, age and personal story. They were asked to memorize their identities and make the person come to life. They were to speak as if they were this individual for the entire class period. As students spent time becoming the identities before them, they were then instructed to become observers. Each student was paired up with another. At the front of the room students sat with a blindfold and had their backs to one another. Students were asked not to reveal their names, religion or country of origin. They were asked to converse about a common assigned topic. While blindfolded students would raise their hand when asked by the instructor if they would likely choose to associate with the other individual. After several minutes of conversation, the two students would remove their blindfold and face one another and reveal their identities. The rest of the class observed and took notes. They were asked to observe body language, awkward silences and key exchanges

Pair 1 Student A and Student B

Student A: Hello there, I am someone who loves to travel and try new restaurants. I am what you might call a foodie. My last trip to California was really amazing—I enjoyed trying the many eateries there.

Student B: Well it is a pleasure to know you. I enjoy traveling myself. I took a road trip with my family last year across several states and found it to be quite fascinating. I also enjoy trying new cuisine!

Student A: Oh that is really cool—so on my bucket list—I have so many places that I hope to visit!

Student B: I also hope to do so.

The instructor then asked the students while blindfolded to raise their hands if they were likely to associate with the other after this initial exchange. They both raised their hands.

The students were then instructed to face one another blind fold removed. Both students revealed their identities.

Student A: I am from Pakistan. I am a 45-year-old man who is a practicing Muslim. I immigrated to the United States 5 years ago and I work as a cab driver.

Student B: I am a White American 30-year-old woman from New Jersey. I am a stay at home mother and have three children.

Pair 2 Student C and Student D

Student C: Hello I am a waitress in a restaurant and I enjoy art. I enjoy visiting museums and like to do paintings.

Student D: I never was able to understand art, but I believe it is a great talent if one were to draw. My children enjoy art and I think it helps them relax and be imaginative.

Student C: Art is a great form of peace.

Student D: Yes peaceful moments are so important in childhood and even in adulthood for that matter.

Student C: Wouldn't it be a great world if there were more peace?

Student D: Yes I agree peace is the way, and we are so far from it.

136 Intermittent Interruptions

Pair 2 also nodded in agreement that they felt that they had something in common and would consider an ongoing discussion.

Student C: Revealed that they were a 25-year-old woman from Paris.

Student D: Revealed their identity as a 24-year-old man who had recently came to Paris as a Syrian refugee. He was working day jobs as a cleaner.

A reaction ensued from both students that this conversation was highly unlikely and that given the terrorist attacks, the animosities and misunderstandings could easily create barriers between them.

Pair 3 Student E and Student F

Student E: I believe God helps all people and that it is important to spread the message of God to others.

Student F: Does God believe we are all equal?

Student E: Yes—God is for all to love and we are all children in the eyes of God—but we must be believers and encourage those that don't believe to do so.

Student F: Is your God better than my God?

Student E: I don't know, I think my God has a good message—to love humankind.

Student F: My God also believes that. I would like for all to believe in my God—and we all should work towards a common humanity.

Student E: But God should be the final objective of all conversations and we should uphold and defend our religion.

The class assumed that the two blindfolded students belonged to a fundamentalist group or even a radical Islamist sect. Student E revealed that she was a 40-year-old Catholic nun and Student F revealed themselves as a 35-year-old Catholic gay male teacher.

The students that developed this activity for class engaged in a large group discussion on how when the blindfolds come off and we reveal the identity markers that we possess, dehumanization begins as barriers go up. Students explained that their main objective was to illustrate the manner human dignity, humanization and human rights can be easily stripped from individuals merely based upon unfounded reactions to stereotypes and biases about the other. Student groups agreed, however that if the blindfolds had never been there, the likelihood of them having a conversation with the other person would not have taken place.

As a follow up to this activity, students were asked to view several personal immigrant stories on TED Talks.

Immigration becomes very convoluted when politics, laws, and presidential candidates of the country become involved, so I lost sight of the individual for a while. While, I haven't been against immigration since high school (conservative Catholic school upbringing), I was surprised how I had separated myself from this issue throughout elections and the rise of Syrian refugees to avoid controversy. But I watched a Tedx Talk in which one immigrant girl said point blank, 'I am afraid of privilege', and I felt like a coward, in a sense, for avoiding controversy. Those words struck a chord in me because the word 'privilege' has been floating around recently as a need. In schools, for example, those who are born into more privileged homes and towns, are more likely to succeed. So, here I have been, ignoring the issue, when this woman who survived countless hardships inside and outside of her country, fears privilege because it harbors the very complacency I've been exuding. While privilege has been seen as something you're lucky to have been born into or achieve, washes away struggle and a need to fight for something. I don't think I'll ever be able to truly relate to immigrant children and their struggle, but I understand it. And I can learn from them.

Many people like to say that we are better than our ancestors, and that we have come so far in terms of being racially unbiased, but I would beg to differ. Just from what I have seen in work, school, and other activities, we are no better than any other century. If someone were to ask me about my ability to relate to immigrant children, I would say I could not. There is no possible way that I could ever understand or relate to the struggles that they have faced. Most people of my background could never understand the struggle of poverty, being in a nation where you cannot even speak their language, or going to school every day and not understand what is being taught only to be looked down upon because of their race, culture, or ethnicity. Today, we live in a society that disrespects anything that strays from the social norm. We become defined by merely one of the things that make up the entirety of who we are, and in a society like that no child will ever be able to thrive.

In several countries, including Syria, Sudan, and Somalia, there is a violent war occurring, in which all resident lives are in danger. The children living in these countries, along with their families, lived in fear of getting attacked or killed, or even kidnapped. There was a fear that if the child attended school, there was a possibility he or she would not return home alive. These residents flee to the nearest refugee camp in a nearby safe country, but the trip is extremely dangerous. The children immigrating to these camps could have witnessed the killing of their parents or siblings, which could have psychological effects on them. Through their long travels, they also could have faced life or death situations themselves, and they could have witnessed the death of their friends. These refugees endured harsh living conditions along their journey; they had a lack of food, water, and no true shelter from weather conditions. The immigrants, especially children, could suffer from PTSD due to their

138 Intermittent Interruptions

experiences. It is important for domestic residents of the new country, especially here in America, to be understanding and supportive of these immigrant children. I would want to help these children and make sure that they are ok and taken care of. If the roles were reversed, I know I would want someone helping me to make sure that I am ok.

Given what I know now, I have much more respect for immigrants. I was truly touched by Tan Le's immigration story. I never knew how scary and hard it was to create a better life. I was truly moved when she said 'like many others my mother carried a bottle of poison in case of pirates and rape. The poison was for me, my sister, grandmother and mother'. For some reason, I feel like I've been so closed minded about immigration and just assumed it was an easy thing. As if risking their lives wasn't hard enough to come to America, once families come to America they have to establish themselves and start new. Watching the Ted Talks made me wonder about my own family and I actually was able to have a discussion with my grandparents about how my great grandmother snuck to America from Lithuania. The article says 'large numbers of immigrant children are experiencing serious problems with education, physical and mental health, poverty, and assimilation into American society'. I believe that as a society we should help immigrants and their families when they come to the United States. Something needs to be done because too many people from the clips gave up everything to come to America, but then struggled because they were in America, but with nothing.

On a more personal note, students also shared their complicated immigrant pathways to the United States and hence brought to bear the contested and complicated identities of students in our classrooms. The embodiment of these contested narratives when erased or forgotten further reminds us how the discourse of the nation-state dilutes and demands homogenous histories and identities.

When my father was around 22 years old, he left India to come to Mexico. From Mexico, he made his way north and managed to sneak past the border and get into the United States. There were many risks involved with this ordeal. Firstly, my dad had to leave my mother and my siblings behind. Secondly, there was no guarantee that he would be able to make it into the United States without being caught and possibly arrested. Fortunately for us, he was able to get in and make a solid living for himself. A few years down the road, he was able to bring my mother and siblings to this country. A few years even further, I was born and enjoyed my birthright citizenship. This narrative is not unique to me. Countless families have ancestors who did very similar things just to ensure that generations of their offspring would never have to deal with the hardships

Intermittent Interruptions   **139**

they dealt with. As I look around today, I see anti-immigrant sentiment. It baffles me to the core because the vast majority of us have ancestors who were immigrants at one point, illegal or otherwise. They all came here with a vision for themselves and their children. An immigrant rarely comes to this country with the intent to harm anyone. That being said, I feel tremendously distraught when my community is a target of hate and anti-immigrant rhetoric. The vast majority of immigration today is centered on hope, not crime. This is why we need to stop this hate against immigrants. It is everyone's consensus that we are much better off if we integrate them into our society.

Another student shared their story and the complex frameworks that shaped their identity.

I am a first generation American and both of my parents are immigrants from El Salvador. They lived there during the time of the Salvadorian Civil War. It was a dangerous time for El Salvador, with the killings and 'disappearances' of many citizens. My mother was a teacher at the time, and teachers were one of the professions of people sought after and assumed to be part of the guerilla, so one of the final pushes for my mother to move to America was when she was taking the bus from a class she was giving to the university, since she was a student as well, and the army had soldiers that pulled over the bus and ordered everyone out and upon seeing her books in the bus ordered everyone in except my mother. She was clearly going to be 'disappeared', but when the brave bus driver, who was a family friend, was ordered to drive away, he told the soldier that he wouldn't leave without her so they eventually let her go. She was so traumatized by that that she went straight home instead of going to class and started to decide that she could no longer live in fear. My father at this point in the war had already graduated as an agronomical engineer and was studying to become a journalist. He got a job at a government facility, but that did not keep him from seeing so many people get shot and killed right in front of him or having corpses fall on him. My father, as a journalist which was another sought after profession thought to be filled with guerilleros, had many close calls, including one where he was almost 'disappeared' because he was charged with treason for not having his papers on him (Salvadorians had to carry specific papers and could be shot instantly if they did not) and being found in possession of books from his Journalist studies for his classes, these including books about communism. He was finally released with the stroke of luck of being allowed a 30 second phone call home (and my grandma didn't answer so he was lucky his aunt answered). This among many other things like family disappearance, crawling the streets wary for mines in search of food during

140 Intermittent Interruptions

battle, attacks on the university while they were in class, and being in fear of recruitment by the army, which was going to schools and recruiting children as young as 12 (and younger), were among the reasons my parents came to the united states. They did not come here to 'steal jobs'. They did not come here to transport drugs. They did not come here as criminals sent out of the country. My parents are both good people who sought to live a life not constantly in fear. It is unfair for people like Donald Trump to look at my family as a by-product of an immigration issue. It is not fair for him to look at my parents, along with other members of my family and family friends who also immigrated and are also honest hardworking people who do in fact pay taxes and didn't hop over any border to gain illegal entry, as the crap of other countries dumped in America. This country was built on immigration.

Syrian Refugee Crisis

One of, if not the greatest, refugee crisis was taking place in Syria. It was also the semester when terrorist attacks took place in Paris and Syrian refugees (as an entire population) took the spotlight as the perpetrators. As I sat in my human rights course, I realized that during this semester in particular it was critical to address the global refugee crisis in Syria. Not much to my surprise, few students were paying attention to the crisis and its global toll. Over the course of the semester, student responses evolved and this highlight the challenges and setbacks that can be faced.

In the early part of the semester, before the Paris terrorist attacks, the Syrian refugee crisis was taking a spotlight in the media. It was important to understand that Syria was experiencing the greatest refugee crisis in history, as an estimated 4 million refugees were seeking safety. Syrians were being referred to as migrants as opposed to refugees and the key question to understand before the simulation/role play was the difference between a refugee and a migrant. These terms were being used interchangeably in the media and were in need of clarification. Migrant implied an individuals' agency to shift from one place to another, whereas refugee clearly implied a violation of human rights and the displacement of people by war and violence. The question of human rights was central to all discussions. Were the rights of the Syrian refugees to be universally embraced or were their rights clearly political, granted in one nation but not in another? Students were also asked to form their own opinions as to whether nations were justified in their rejection of refugees in their nations. To begin this lesson, the class was broken into countries. Students represented Germany, Hungary, USA, Gulf Nations, Turkey and Syrian refugees and a Human Rights NGO. Students were charged with developing a stance for an in-class role play/debate. They were to speak as leaders of the nations and develop a list of actions and policies that they had enacted towards Syrian refugees.

Students who were Syrian refugees were to create a personal narrative around their migrant journey.

Students formed into their respective groups and faced one another in a round table discussion. I will share some highlights from the debate to illustrate the critical dialogue that developed from this role play simulation activity.

The Syrian refugee group opened the debate forum with their story.

Student S1:

> We are Syrian refugees and we are formerly trained doctors. My wife and I are seeking a better life—we fear for our lives, our futures and our safety. We plead of you to allow us to come into your nations and share our skills and knowledge. We bring with us great enthusiasm to grow and integrate into your communities. If we had a choice, we would have never left our beautiful nation. We have watched friends and family members be mercilessly killed. There are no functioning structures left. For the sake of humanity and your sympathy, please allow us to make your country great.

Student S2:

> I am a poor craftsmen. I worked hard to establish a good life for my family. I come with my three children. My wife was killed in Syria. I bring nothing with me only my humility to have a safe life. My children and I desire simple basics, safety, food and the right to live. Please understand our cause.

The "nations" at the roundtable listened as the Syrian refugees pleaded their case. Their responses were to be positioned according the national policies of their given nations.

Hungary was the first to respond to reflect the present crisis at the train stations.

Student H:

> We empathize with your situation, but we cannot possibly allow for your stay in our nation. Our nation is small, and cannot withstand pressures of social integration and welfare of refugees. We fear terrorists amongst your masses. Our belief is your cultural beliefs may serve to be incompatible with ours.

Turkey followed the conversation.

Student T:

> Turkey has been at the forefront of refugee adoption—we urge other nations here to follow our example. This is a humanitarian crisis.

142 Intermittent Interruptions

Germany then interjected into the conversation to challenge other nations to follow their agenda.

Student G:

> Germany is the nation that is at the forefront of inviting refugees to their nations. Please allow in a humane and peaceful way for refugees to pass through your borders to reach our border. European nations must uphold shengen—or open border policies. The EU must come together as a united front. Our goal is to bring in refugees in vast numbers and allow them to integrate into our nation.

Student G then challenged other nations such as Gulf Nations to interject as well as USA.

Student U:

> The United States has historically taken refugees, and we believe we have been proactive. Our president has just signed to allow more refugees into our borders. We believe we have done our part and we believe European nations need to build an alliance on this issue. You must treat refugees with respect and please refrain from treating them like criminals.

Gulf Nations had an argument that they would not accept physical bodies yet would be willing to provide financial aid.

Student GN:

> We share the culture and religion of our fellow Syrian refugees, yet we fear terrorism and we will provide aid to help in the situation. We never signed the 1951 Refugee Convention.

UN NGO interjected

Student NGO:

> We are getting reports of inhumane treatment of refugees. Labeling refugees by numbers, tricking them, no food, no water. Containing them at train stations. Kicking their families by reporters. Gulf Nations never signed 1951 Refugee Convention. Does this document hold any power to enforce nations?

Syrian students

Student S1:

> Yes we can share with you that this is what we have experienced—we are being treated like criminals. We are only hoping that you can see that we are not here by choice—we were forced.

As can be observed from student interactions, there is clearly a pattern of mis-understanding and criminalizing of refugees. As the debate ensued, a clear pattern emerged with Syrian refugees, Germany and the Human Rights NGO attempting to clarify with Hungary, Gulf Nations and USA on the importance of understanding the global crisis. The human rights question was central to this debate and the ongoing discussion was whether fear of terrorism and national policies could be viewed as valid reasons to deny humane treatment and assistance to refugees.

The class was asked to reconvene at the end of the semester in order to reassess the shifts in national agendas after the Paris terrorist attacks, given the greater scrutiny on Syrian refugees. Were French airstrikes in Syria and the growing resistance to refugees justified from the point of view of peace and human rights activists? Students grappled with difficult discussions about the link of terrorism with the influx of refugees. Students were engaged in a follow-up activity was to provide the students with another lens to observe global events.

The classroom was divided into six distinct spaces. Large sheets of paper were posted in the walls with different terms listed on each. The terms humanity, terrorism, peace, hate, power and dignity were posted around the classroom. Students were asked to define what they were, understand the interplay of these concepts and further create a diagram that would illustrate the clashes and connections between them. The first task was to write down statements and ideas related to each general concept. Student commentaries were as follows.

Groups were then asked to do a gallery walk and explore one another's posters.

HUMANITY	TERRORISM	PEACE
Human rights	9/11	No war, no fear
Peace	ISIS	Harmony
Acceptance	Fear	Global connectivity
Respect for one another	Paris Attacks	Cooperation
No war	Power	
Justice	Evil	
	Violence	
HATE	POWER	DIGNITY
Terrorism	Money	Humane treatment
Genocide	Religion	Human rights for all
Crime	Government	Freedom of expression—
Islamophobia	Law enforcement	freedom to exist and be
Discrimination	Corruption	yourself
Holocaust	Media	Gender equality
Collective identities	Ignorance	Civil disobedience
Racism	Nationalism	

144 Intermittent Interruptions

They were also asked to underline concepts that were similar to their group's ideas and to challenge possible ideas. Overall, the class was in agreement with the statements that were developed. Discussions began to spark, however, in regard to the ideas of peace, humanity and dignity. The class was skeptical to the pie in the sky ideas for a perfect world. This was an important moment to discuss.

The group responsible for Power stated the following:

> Power is the strongest group here since we control all aspects of the global order.

In strong agreement, students working on Hate stated:

> Hate follows power and hence terrorism—this keeps dignity, humanity, and peace at bay.

The rest of the class was encouraged to join the discussion and develop a critical understanding of the statements that were asserted.

The Humanity and Peace group joined forces to debate with the other groups.

> If hate and terror were inevitable, the world would have ended in a nuclear disaster at this point. There is a natural gravitation back towards elements of peace, dignity and humanity in every point of history.

At this point, the class engaged in further discussion related to Examples 8.1 through 8.3.

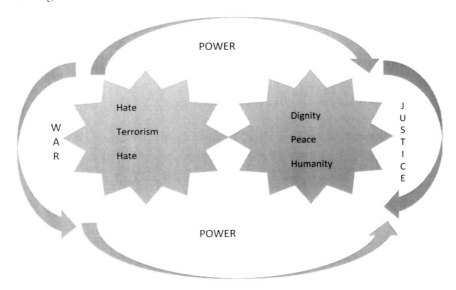

EXAMPLE 8.1 This image describes the omnipresence of power and the circular nature of power leading to war when it lacks dignity, peace and humanity.

Intermittent Interruptions **145**

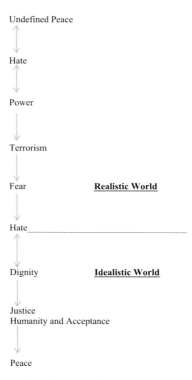

EXAMPLE 8.2 This group described a realistic vs an idealistic world in relation to undefined peace and peace. Hate, power, fear and terrorism were defined as leading to an undefined peace.

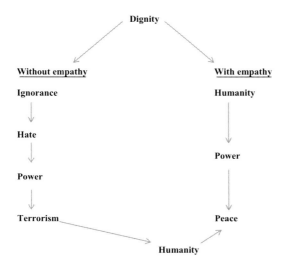

EXAMPLE 8.3 This image uses Dignity as a central driving force and when dignity lacks empathy they illustrate the likelihood of hate and power leading to terrorism.

146 Intermittent Interruptions

The challenge to grapple with these concepts required a deep philosophical engagement with particular ideas related to global citizenship. Understanding the incredible oppression of power of hate as a precursor to terror and war led many students to express a sense of entrapment and frustration. This frustration was very real and the lack of "faith" in humanity and possibilities of peace became very raw. In particular, students were being bombarded by messages daily given the current day politics surrounding the Paris terror attacks. The debate was not in a vacuum or in regard to hypothetical scenarios. Perhaps that is what created a sense of limitation. But ultimately, it was a reminder that such frustration does not merely justify choosing hate and ignorance.

These moments in the classroom are where the educator must play a role in not only allowing students to voice their frustrations and questions, but to also leave the possibility that there may not be a resolve or solution at hand. The moment requires both student and teacher alike to know that the exercise of understanding these concepts is the "teachable moment" in itself. As a follow up to the exercise, students were asked to reflect on Stephen Hopgood's (2015) assertion about the End Times of Human Rights. Students were asked to respond to a statement about the future of human rights being a dawn or a sunset.

Student responses to the question:

> The world's combination of apathy and lack of empathy is the deteriorating force or human rights and activism—social media has created a passive activism—yet the act stops there and does not extend to an act of humanitarianism. Social media also preaches hate, and that voice is speaking as loudly, if not louder than those preaching peace.
>
> We need to begin the conversation about human rights at the beginning of children's lives in school. Schools need to make them important. If we are hard wired to believe in rights—maybe we would view mankind differently.
>
> Politics, power and money = sunset of human rights.
>
> As long as someone, somewhere stands up for someone–human rights are still alive.
>
> One man's terrorist is another man's freedom fighter.
>
> Human rights activists, are everyday people like you and I–that's where we will always make a difference and uphold the dignity of others. Many activists do as much as they can to support universal human rights but they are the worlds most silenced voice.
>
> We need to dismantle the human rights industry—that is now attached to political power and money—human rights are not a commodity to be sold.
>
> There are simultaneously in every moment a win and a loss for human rights. We legalized gay marriage in America—but then we reject Syrian refugees in Europe. There will never be all wins—but we have to take the wins as signs that human rights will always be part of the conversation.

This not the a sunset for human rights activists, this is the thunder you hear that keeps you up at night, and the rain will try to drown out the noise, but it will always turn into dawn.

This exercise was provided to allow students to further digest the very serious discussions we were having. It was important to discuss questions such as: What are moral absolutes? How is good and evil defined? What is the need for collective identity and what is the motivating force of extremists? By understanding historical roots of terrorism and hate, students began to have a deeper nuanced reaction, rather than the knee jerk response and as critical global citizens they were able to create a more complex lens of understanding.

One of the key moments that I take away from my students during our unofficial lessons is that students have been underexposed to many ideas related to dehumanization.

There is an underlying passive acceptance of the status quo and little interrogation or personal introspection in relation to more difficult questions related to human rights, democracy and global citizenship. It's a sad reminder of the many moments that have escaped the K–12 classroom to engage in pedagogies of resistance and interruption.

I would like to end this chapter with a few highlights of one particular *learner-actor* that has become a critical peace activist. These learner activists have become the voice for those who have had their voices taken by human rights violations. One particular student of mine became inspired to become a critical peace activist and forge a grassroots movement. Through engaging in a politics of interruption as a global citizen, she is making an impact at local and global levels. Natu Suzie Kure became an outspoken activist against Boko Haram and a staunch supporter of the Bring Back Our Girls Movement. Years after graduating, Natu came back as a guest speaker in my class and the words that resonated strongly with the students were "This is real!" She was rightly referring to the tourist nature of understanding about global crises and issues. She reminded the class that social media allows us to be engaged and express solidarity or concern, but it becomes a mere spectacle at that. It is when we as humans can come to the realization that these human rights atrocities are real and not sensationalized media. Can we move forward to disrupt these acts? Natu has not abandoned the project to bring back the girls despite setbacks and hindrances.

Natu reflected on her personal development as an activist:

> I have always been an activist but on the low not like now. I guess probably because I was not able to get organization or groups to work with when I was back in Nigeria and I was scared to do it alone (maybe). But when I moved to the states and got accepted at the university it was a different ball game. When I took human right classes and enrolled as a

148 Intermittent Interruptions

> peace studies minor, there I was made to disbelieve the African proverb that says *'A tree cannot make a forest'*; in my own words it taught me yes a tree cannot make a forest but *'it can make a shade'*.

Her source of inspiration is connected to the exposure to peace and human rights curriculum.

> Peace Studies was my number [one] source of inspiration on this journey and I will do it again anytime anywhere. I learned to be the change I want to see in the world (and that is the journey I have embarked on). I have learned to never hide my story because it might inspire someone. I have learned to be a face of hope and inspiration. I have learned never to give up on peace and hope. And the list goes on and on, but am forever grateful for my peace studies classes and professors.

Natu speaks passionately about her personal connection to the Bring Back Our Girls Movement in Nigeria. Natu initially worked with the United Nations mission in Nigeria, but was disheartened by the lack of direct impact with the work she was doing with the UN.

> I had the opportunity to do 15-month long internship with the Nigerian Mission to the United Nations and I worked with the Fourth Committee (Special Political and decolonization committee, it also deals with peacekeeping, mine action, outer space, public information). Through my service, I was able to understand that the UN cannot function without the member states. Regardless of whatever decisions they have to make there must be a majority agreement no matter how important it is—if the member states don't agree then it won't be taken into effect. People are dying every day, but the UN cannot take immediate action because of bureaucracy and that really hurt me. Those experiences got me thinking about what and how we can help without waiting for the UN. I love diplomacy—it's something I always wanted to do but I want to do something that will impact those that need it directly. And that is the reason why I took it upon myself to be a carrier of peace, work with the local community and help people create a voice and take action beforehand and not wait around while the government gets done with the paper work.

Natu then continued to forge forward with her grassroots work that is directly related to the Bring Back Our Girls Movement.

> I wouldn't take a lot of credit for the BBOG (Bring Back Our Girls) movement because I believe I should have not done as much as I should have done. I have participated on a few events but it is a struggle because

the Nigerian government isn't helping. But the reason why this is so dear to me is because I am human first of all, then like a woman like those girls, then from Nigeria again like them, then from Northern Nigeria too like them, so this could be me or any member of my family who was abducted. And I guess if it were my family members I won't sit back and watch I will be there in Nigeria fighting and that's why I can't stop. The important part of this all that I want people to know is, more than 2000 women and girls have been kidnapped from 2013 to date. Been raped and used as suicide bombers against their wish. The lucky ones were able to escape and the unlucky ones have been killed with bombs, the unfortunate ones are sex slaves of the terrorists. It's just heart breaking knowing I have cousins, nephews and nieces of that age and I can't survive knowing they are going through that. But so much is going on behind doors. I will be travelling to Chibok this summer.

Natu expresses her dismay and struggle as someone who is deeply committed to resist the plight and tragedy of these women who have been abducted and utilized as weapons of war. Natu keeps this story alive despite the fact that the media has moved on from the initial headlines in regard to Boko Haram and the victimization of girls. Recently reports by BBC News and the New York Times about the abducted girls have been highlighted in the news, yet the ongoing dialogue is where Natu demands awareness and perseveres. The news articles report on a live video sent by Boko Haram of the kidnapped girls, yet in the write-up the sense of urgency and tragedy seems diluted and leaves the reader largely with the impression that these girls look "well fed" and seem not to be "in distress". Through the work of Natu as a speaker and activist, she reminds us that "this is real" and we must craft an ongoing dialogue with civil society and governments to resist dehumanization. Natu's process is in continuous transformation as she seeks grassroots avenues of resistance and transformation and reconfigures her strategies in the face of setbacks and challenges. Her enduring journey characterizes the meaningful transformative sites where possibilities for change arise when learners occupy them and become the critical peace activists.

CONCLUSION

Now Is the Time to Begin

> Knowledge emerges only through invention and re-invention through restless, impatient, continuing hopeful inquiry human beings pursue in the world, with the world, and with each other.
>
> —Paulo Freire

The multiple narratives in this book have provided an intimate view into classroom and community spaces, where possibilities for peace have been cultivated and collective dialogues have disrupted multiple forms of symbolic violence. In sharp contrast to the oversimplified common classroom space that is in many ways shut off from the world, alternatives have been showcased. The work of these teacher activists is in every way a small victory over dominant forms that curtail creativity and radical work in the everyday classroom setting. Yet an understanding about the assault on schools, teachers and the nature of localized battles can leave little incentive to reach beyond the confines of one's neighborhood school. We face a great turning point in the education debate as we encounter the common core standards, annual testing regimes and changing teacher preparation and evaluation criteria. We additionally face a world that is increasingly violent and unsettled.

Let me share an example that elucidates an ineffectual battle over contested spaces that oftentimes has hidden winners and losers. Thinking back to my experience as a teacher in an urban school and refusing to take the test as a symbolic peaceful protest, I have mixed feelings when understanding undercurrents of the present-day opt-out movement. Let's take, for example, the current framing of the testing opt-out movement in Long Island, New York. Long Island has the most segregated counties in the nation with approximately 125 school districts and 656 public schools. These districts are segregated along lines of race and class and many are grossly entrenched in structures of exclusion. I would like to highlight an aspect of this movement, namely the unusual alliances that form under the cloud of "resistance", that perhaps lead us back to the same winners and losers. It feels like the newest game in town is "the opt out movement". Being part of the movement has become an act of "civil disobedience" or "taking back" our schools from the demons in the distance. Case in point, there is nothing alluring about the assault on teachers, students and communities in the current age of reform agendas and policies. There are, however, undertones of unusual alliances in the efforts of the "take back our schools" movement. Perhaps it would be appropriate to take back our schools had we realized equity and access to students of all backgrounds regardless of race or class. Yet "taking back our schools" to reinstitute segregated districts based on class and racial makeup is counterproductive and attacks the very core of a democratic society. Tying test scores and teacher livelihood together is outrageous yet tying test scores to segregation and exclusionary housing policies is just as outrageous.

Opting out of tests resonates with principles of participatory democracy such as my experience over a decade ago, yet providing the option to "opt out" of school districts that are failing in order to integrate diverse students is abhorred. These very same individuals pay upwards of thousands of dollars for college gateway exam preparation and essentially "opt in" to that requirement. Wouldn't resistance and opting out of the college gateway exams serve to strengthen the movement of civil disobedience? Or would that be too risky? I neither have the intention to minimize these very core debates nor am I romantic about any easy solutions to the problems at hand. I do, however, wish to illustrate how we spiral back to the same point of departure as we balance the wins and gains.

This is where my deep-seated discomfort lies—in these very real contradictions and hypocritical stances. Segregated by race and class, the new common core aligned tests resulted in lowered scores in all districts and threatened the ownership of high test scores that has become the entitlement of districts that separate themselves from others. These highly guarded physical boundaries are further exacerbated by real estate housing practices that clearly separate these communities from the "Other". Commonly accepted notions of "moving" to "those districts" on the island to ensure that "those kids don't attend with mine" mimic racism and violence. The message to underprivileged students becomes that their lives don't matter and that we as a society have very little invested in their future. The politics are dangerous and have appeal yet they also come at what costs? Do the blinders come back on when trying to provide necessary interventions and resources for low-income minority youth if funding is withheld for failure to comply with testing requirements? Is the opt-out movement occupied by individuals who seek to preserve their entitlement and

152 Conclusion

privilege and their segregated neighborhoods? Resistance comes with a price with gains only for those that already have access to networks of upward social mobility. Not only do we risk some gains for low-income districts, we sever the link to college readiness and gainful employment.

Linda Darling Hammond (2010) makes that argument that "given the critical importance of education for individual and societal success in the flat world we now inhabit, inequality in the provision of education is an antiquated tradition the United States can no longer afford" (p. 327). Where there is less faith in the value of education as a prime vehicle for upward mobility, we lose countless individuals to disengagement and dropping out. This is violence in all forms-systemic, institutional, socio-political and cultural. Once again, those that will benefit from education and necessary skills for gainful employment will acquire what is needed, whether they opt out or opt in-as has historically been the case.

Looking at the current storm of debate facing schools, it becomes difficult to believe there can be any real victories or hope for critical peace educators. The emotionally charged polarization around schools, teachers, curriculum and students is uncomfortable and leaves one to wonder what happens when the school doors close and children begin their day under the standards of common core and the shadows of No Child Left Behind. Is there a silver lining for them? Can teachers occupy the current terrain of teaching and provide opportunities for our students to grow as socially responsible global citizens and peace activists? Can unofficial curriculums become the moments of teaching for peace and democracy? But what about the countless efforts of individuals who resist those messages for students and send a counter message to students that they do matter and they will take every opportunity to buffer them against the forces that oppress them? Can a curriculum engage students in conversations about feeling deeply embedded and connected to humanity both locally and globally?

Lisa Delpit (2013), in her book, *Multiplication is for White People*, expresses her anger at many issues related to schools and she further poses ten things that must be in place to foster excellent urban schools. Number ten on her list reads as follows: "Foster a sense of children's connection to community, to something greater than themselves". A connection to something "greater than themselves" can perhaps be the journey to conscientization. These acts take place both locally and globally and solving global issues will require vastly innovative ideas that perhaps are cultivated when critical and collaborative thinking is nurtured and awakened in young minds. The question then becomes, what is the path to shaping peace activists and critical global citizens? It begins with a keen awareness of relations of power, oppression and the value of human dignity. Such awareness is ever more pressing in the current political and global climate of fear, terrorism, racist nativism and isolationism. Awareness, hence, follows with a politics of interruption and with pedagogies of resistance. Yet, their work remains unfinished until these ideas are connected with the contexts of real lives.

Educators must teach students that they are part of a globalized world, a much larger system than what they may know locally. These goals of citizenship education are inconsistent with the citizen's role in a global world today because many people have multiple national commitments and live in multiple nation-states. Nonetheless, the development of citizens with global and cosmopolitan identities and commitments is contested in nation-states throughout the world because nationalism remains strong. Nationalism and globalization coexist in tension worldwide (Benhabib 2004; Castles and Davidson 2000). When responding to the problems wrought by international migration, schools in multicultural nation-states must deal with complex educational issues in ways consistent with their democratic ideologies and declarations. There is a broad divide between the democratic ideals in Western nations, teacher practice, curriculum and daily experiences of students in schools (Banks 2004a). Ethnic minority students in the United States, Canada, the United Kingdom, Germany and France—as in other nations throughout the world—often experience discrimination because of their cultural, linguistic, religious and value differences. Often, both students and teachers identify these students as the "Other".

Educating through an ethnocentric lens prevents deep engagement with globalization and cultural difference since ethnocentrism restricts inquiry beyond what is known locally. The goal of citizenship education should be to help students initially disrupt dehumanization and oppression and further develop an identity and attachment to the global community and a human connection to people around the world. The United Nations Universal Declaration on Human Rights outlines thirty points of dignity for all human beings. These points of dignity represent one's natural born rights that apply universally despite national and geographic borders. A discussion of such rights is at most a fleeting thought, and rarely a deep engagement of what it means to share responsibility for others and uphold ones right and those of fellow humanity. To truly understand the value of human rights and dignity, individuals must grapple with self-introspection about their sense of entitlement to various rights that they believe they possess. As has been previously argued, human rights have also been appropriated to enforce domination and violence as well and demand careful analysis. Beginning as such, this platform can then serve as a basis for a powerful conversation about the value of humanity, dignity and social justice in both the local and global arena.

By making the oppression of students within and outside the classroom relevant, students can learn about empathy and social justice towards one another. Students should be empowered by the understanding that they can make a difference and ought to engage in activism and human rights projects. Students must also develop a deep understanding of the need to take action as citizens

154 Conclusion

of the global community and make decisions to help solve the world's complex problems. Essentially, social movements are where change can begin. In the current political climate, my students felt stalled when discussing issues related to the assault on women, immigrants and the racialized body. The politicized nature and the raw anger and hate related to "how to solve the world's problems" are pervading their social media landscape. Violence again is being touted as the means to achieve peace in our community, nation and world with clear parameters of whose body to include and exclude, and whose can be violated and whose can remain safe. This silence and the resistance to listen to other viewpoints are resoundingly deaf. Yet, teacher and learner activists must continue to be radical and work towards respect, equality and social justice in their cultural communities, nations, and regions and in the world.

Global identities, attachments and commitments constitute cosmopolitanism (Nussbaum 2002). Cosmopolitans view themselves as citizens of the world who will make decisions and take actions in the global interests that will benefit humankind. Nussbaum states that their "allegiance is to the worldwide community of human beings" (p. 4). According to Appiah, "in the last few centuries, as every human community has gradually been drawn into a single web of trade and a global network of information, we have come to a point where each of us can realistically imagine contacting any other of our six billion or so fellow humans and sending that person something worth having ... unfortunately we can now also send, through negligence, as easily as malice, things that will cause harm—a virus, an airborne pollutant, a bad idea" (Appiah p. 5). Global citizenship education should help students to realize that "no local loyalty can ever justify forgetting that each human being has responsibilities to every other" (Appiah 2006 p. xvi). A *differentiated* conception of citizenship, rather than a universal one, is needed to help marginalized groups attain civic equality and recognition in multicultural democratic nations (Young 1989). Many problems result from a universal notion of citizenship according to which "citizenship status transcends particularity and difference" and "laws and rules are blind to individual and group differences" (Young 1989 p. 250). It is equally imperative to bridge the study of "domestic multiculturalism" to the international arena and globalization. Across the board, our curriculums are deeply, globally disconnected. Creating those global connections, establishing the study of peace and human rights, and teaching for social justice can reveal limitless opportunities for students.

It is not until we make it essential to consider ourselves part of a globalized world that we can begin to personally define global citizenship. Providing youth with an opportunity to develop a sense of responsibility towards other human beings could serve as an ideal platform for deeper discussions about oppression and social justice. Critical and democratically conscious teaching and learning practices can have a positive impact with far-reaching implications for social action. Painting a more accurate picture of what is happening in the world and understanding the complexity of issues such as terrorism, human rights violations, immigration and cultural difference are integral to achieving this goal. Yet the limited resources and prescriptive curriculum of most schools require educators to be creative in engaging students in such discussions through reaching out to organizations, developing service learning projects and bringing activists into schools. It is important to encourage students to search for facts and challenge their own assumptions. Addressing student fears and encouraging them to think about ways to engage in global understanding form important elements of such pedagogy. Building a vision for peaceful coexistence and encouraging students to be futurists, where they envision a nonviolent world, is important. What is required is teacher initiative to educate for fairness and equity, to value difference and recognize injustice and then to take action. Everyone plays a role in this process. There is hope when teachers care and come together to face these issues head on. As with every student in our classroom, we have a grave responsibility as educators to make every effort to reach each student. This is the task that we must continually strive for and incorporate into our teaching practices. Children in these schools became "critical readers". As we are reminded by the words of Michael Apple (2007):

> Those committed to a participatory curriculum understand that knowledge is socially constructed, that it is produced and disseminated by people who have particular values, interests and biases. This is simply a fact of life, since all of us are formed by our cultures, genders, geographies and so on. In a democratic curriculum, however, young people learn to be "critical readers" of their society. When confronted with some knowledge or viewpoint, they are encouraged to ask questions like: Who said this? Why did they say it? Why should we believe this? Who benefits if we believe this and act upon it? (p. 151)

By answering these questions posed by Apple, a transformative process can begin as students begin to understand their rights and become inspired to advocate for others. A school-wide commitment to humanize education would require educators to play a critical role in bringing the community and the world into the classroom and expecting students to engage with them in deeply critical and serious ways. Rosaldo (1997) has asserted that citizenship identity and rights are not afforded equally to all members of society, regardless of their legal citizenship status. Within a history of global inequalities leading to the displacement and exodus of people, many migrants and immigrants act as social and civic citizens insofar as they contribute to the sociocultural and economic fabric of the nation in which they reside. Institutions normalize the citizenship identity of some subjects while subjugating others, depriving them of social and human rights. Can rights be realized and affirmed with one's engagement with conscientization, revolutionary practice and solidarity with

156 Conclusion

victims? This utopian project of Paulo Freire addresses the need for a fundamental faith in human dialogue and community. Freire argues that authentic revolutionary praxis is utopian in nature, which means that it is harmonious, reflective, dynamic, reflective and dialogical. Paulo Freire (1985) also reminds us, "to be utopian is not to be merely idealistic or impractical but to engage in denunciation and annunciation" (p. 57). Based on Freirean dialogical praxis, this denunciation through which teachers and learners examine and critique the "dehumanizing reality" of the world, combined with the annunciation of a theory of action—one that is not mere rhetoric but "an historic commitment" to change—offers not only the foundation for action, but the vital sense of hope needed to generate that action. Exploding the myths can allow for reconciliation. Notions of normalized citizenship serve to divide communities and strip away opportunities to allow for serious dialogue about transnationality and globalization. Through validating student thoughts and transforming the classroom space into sites of debate, analysis, problem solving and activism, students understand that their ideas have power. We need to believe that students can make a difference, become global citizens, that they can be part of social movements and that they are a powerful and influential segment of society. The spaces between Otherness and belonging can be embraced by educators and provide ample opportunity for learners to be guided and nurtured to not only define selves, but to open up the discussion to the larger classroom to understand how they are implicated in the dialogue as well.

The thought that critical peace education may become mainstreamed into teacher education programs is fleeting at most. The narratives that have been presented in this book reify the marginal nature of critical peace pedagogy. Ideally if such unofficial lessons were to become central to teacher training curriculum, I contemplate what the outcomes might be. As learning and curriculum have become increasingly quantified and product based, the openings for peace praxis seem more difficult to create and maintaining the authentic nature of critical peace praxis is vital. Edward Brantmeier (2011) states that the challenges to mainstreaming critical peace education stem from a history of "peace" being politically suspect and the outcome based policy of schools that decenters power away from teachers and classrooms. Brantmeier provides us with the following insight as well:

> Moving from marginal or implicit to mainstream peace education in teacher education is also central to this paradigm shift. The complexities of the concepts of peace and the theoretical frameworks of peace thinking need to be incorporated into teacher education rhetoric and courses to deepen the causes of social justice that already exist via implied peace education in mainstream teacher education. Linkages and dialogue between mainstream teacher education and peace education need to become more frequent, acceptable in the eyes of mainstream teacher

education, and promoted by local universities to ensure the exposure and strengthening of peace education, both explicit and implied. Particularly, explicit peace education in teacher education needs to become a normal rather than a rare phenomenon.

(2011 pp. 370–31)

Although schools continue to be the playing fields of failed reforms and policies I have elucidated the manner students are being exposed to critical peace education through an "unofficial curriculum" that can be interruptive and rich with discussions about dignity, social justice and human rights. These powerful moments become the critical stepping-stones of authentic self-reflection that can ultimately serve as the beginning of educating youth for participatory global citizenship. Collectively, they form a grassroots movement that mobilizes around deeply political meanings, critical interrogations and disruptions of local and global society. Words of inspiration from Maxine Greene (2005) encourage us as well,

> For those of us who sadly say that there "are no causes anymore," it may be important for teachers themselves to recapture some of the great campaigns of the past: the struggles for civil rights, for women's rights, for human rights, none of which have been fully achieved. Again it is a matter of imagining a future in full awareness of approximations and uncertainties and even the likelihood of failure. Still, if we can retain our freedoms, we still (and this can be made clear to students) have the capacity to choose.

(2005 p. 79)

Returning to my classroom from that Fall afternoon, the moments of silence were difficult to navigate yet Sue Lingenfelter, with all her determination, then asked my class, "Now that you know about the horrors of child sex trafficking, what are you going to do?" She answered her own question for them and spoke about how her life is now defined by the work she does to combat human trafficking. Sue further went on to tell the class of her experience visiting the Love 146 Round Home in the Philippines where rescued victims of child trafficking were provided survivor care. With tears in her eyes, Sue told the class that she, along with her fellow activists, were given a standing ovation from the little girls at the Round Home. The children saw them as heroes. Sue reminded the class that she was no hero, but rather these young girls who had faced the darkest atrocities of humanity who had the will and courage to believe they could live a life of peace and hope were the true heroes. There are stories of young victims that have been able to prosecute those that enslaved them, other survivors have become leading activists and yet others have married in the face of cultural shaming and exclusion and have found normalcy within their lives. Sue again told the class that activism can be as simple as telling one more person about these dark realities to make human trafficking more than a

158 Conclusion

"media moment" and this is symbolic in that you choose to spread knowledge and awareness. Throughout the past several years, my students have approached Sue with ideas for activism; there have been Justice Jams, Bowl-a-thons, Walk-a-thons and social media campaigns. The lives of these young victims matter and we demand that they matter, for human dignity should not be a choice. As an educator, I chose to "open" rather than "shut" my classroom doors to the dark crises that face humanity and further create an opening for some possible symbolic disruption of violence.

> DARKNESS
> Our lives are coming to an end as our future is vague
> We will die from this sickly plague
> Our houses are burnt and our hopes are shattered
> Our clothes torn and our belongings battered
> Our lives are fading—love is failing
> The world is now corrupt, a dark boat is sailing
> The trees are withered and dried
> There is no wind, sun, or tide
> Not even air or water we are given
> The earth is mad and by hate it is driven
> (5th grade student)

Many of us now find ourselves facing a giant metaphorical abyss standing at the edge of a cliff as undeniable movements of the world appear to be going in reverse and we sense a free flowing downward spiral. These are the many images that come to mind as I digest the new era of undemocratic and painfully violent ideological forms that are upon us. The era of Trump politics has called to question the meaning of nationhood and has made vulnerable the fault lines that exist within civil rights mobilizations. The assault on identity politics and the divisions within civil and human rights movements hint at the challenges that need to be addressed. For example, privilege and power coupled with feminism has spurred the commodity feminist who has little in common with radical grassroots latina and black feminist movements. The commodification of rights, as has been the case with peace and diversity initiatives, has led to the counterproductive question of whose rights matter more, yours or mine? Further, when I can use privilege and power to assert my rights, those rights become more important than yours. Such discourse endangers the intent to secure symbolic widespread disruption for all members in a movement in order to preserve the privilege of a few. These are dangerous developments for fragile mobilizations that are now forced to restrategize and refocus their ideological assumptions. Alternatively, the Right nationalist movement capitalized on fear, anger and hate in order to gain popularity, where unlikely unities were forged between groups like blue collar workers and corporate executives.

White populist rage, white hegemony or the alt-right movement has threatened to upend decades of work that have fragile structures in place to uphold the dignity of the most vulnerable members of our society. Folded into a nativist nationalism is the agenda to secure a "white" dominance in all facets of civil life—a "white-lash" is occurring at the growing multicultural and globalized world that we live in. The economic woes of these individuals are viewed through a lens of xenophobia and racism-simultaneously the elimination of such threats can only serve to make their nation "great" again. The moral crisis where it becomes "safe to hate" has triggered one of the greatest escalations in bullying and hate crimes in schools and communities. Children in their classrooms are echoing racist, sexist and homophobic language as they absorb hateful language and mimic Trump rhetoric and enraged tirades from his supporters. The weight of the rhetoric that is wrapped up in a revival of violent historical xenophobia demands that educators provide children with a serious discussion of history. When children hear about the Ku Klux Klan, a ban on Muslims or building a wall to stop Mexicans, we are obligated to teach them about the facts and provide avenues of constructive discussion and critical dialogue to disrupt hate. Teachers are feeling blindsided on how to handle an emotionally and negatively charged classroom and these struggles only further reveal the gaps that have been left by the "normalcy of complacency". The weak response to interrupt bullying and the lack of response from teachers is revealing. Once again there are the "we all get along" lesson plans being shared amongst teachers and the one day "peace lesson". Yes, this is another reminder of the superficial engagement that exists when understanding violence and its impact on student's lives. We fail to give students the tools, both short and long term, to understand and process how violence in its overt and covert forms is oppressive and threatening. The task becomes more challenging when children assert that "peace" can only be achieved by eliminating groups of people from society. These assertions need to be deconstructed in the classroom as well. Superficial one-day lessons on peace are counterproductive in that they become an attempt to wash over and silence the unrest. And peace, as it remains undefined, is not achieved when children disengage from school, their communities and lives.

When Donald Trump won the American presidency, far right French politician Jean Marine Le Pen stated, "Nothing is immutable. What has happened this night is not the end of the world, it's the end of a world" (The Telegraph 11/9/16). Le Pen is perhaps applauding the global isolationist and insular agendas muted by Trump. Throughout history, nations have opened and closed their borders, however, the renewed welcoming of global fractures and tight restrictive borders based on the politics of nativism and exclusion reverses the notions of global citizenship as has been defined in the last part of the century. What does it now mean to belong? And where does one believe they are to belong? If the message continues to be that there is no longer a notion of a cooperative and open global landscape, but rather a fractured and hostile autonomy of segregated nations, the idea of global citizenship risks being undone. This moment in time has yet to be defined. The pressure to become a segregated, hostile and violent world can define this moment, or it can be counter-defined within its current framework with creative and renewed peaceful solutions. Perhaps the fractures, ugliness and hate may remind people that achieving human rights first begins in our own backyard. Our violent "peaceful democracies" need to be redefined, to be held accountable and be responsive to all members of civil society. If we interrupt hate in our classrooms, our daily interactions and in our local communities, we again forge possibilities for peace. This task will not be easy, perhaps it may be one of the greatest turning points in history.

Collectively, I imagine what the possibilities might be if we were to begin the process of transformation with educators who feel responsible and are deeply committed to critical peace praxis. If our discourse had been actively engaged in countering violence, might we have been better equipped to resist the current rise of hate in our classrooms? Going forward, who might these individuals be who "make critical" the official curriculum and further engage in political activist projects in their schools and communities to overcome dehumanization. Might this result in a larger collective of informed and critical citizens who are prepared to interrupt violence and complicated hegemonic forms in their daily lives and restore dignity universally? It may only be at that moment where we could potentially begin to have a conversation about the nature of "peace" in place of merely imagining the possibilities of "peace". In reality, nevertheless, there will never be such a moment. And what sets the teacher and learner activists in this book apart is, in spite of it all, they understand profoundly that there is no better time than now to occupy the margins to act in deeply radical, political and critical ways.

REFERENCES

Akintunde, O. (2006). Diversity.Com: Teaching an Online Course on White Racism and Multiculturalism. *Multicultural Perspective* 8(2), 35–45.

Appiah, K. A. (2006). Cosmopolitanism: Ethnics in a World of Strangers. New York: Norton.

Apple, M. (1995). Education and Power. New York and London: Routledge.

Apple, M. (1996). Cultural Politics and Education. New York: Teachers College Press.

Apple, M. (2004). Ideology and Curriculum. New York and London: Routledge Press.

Apple, M. & Beane, J. (2007). Democratic Education: Second Edition Lessons in Powerful Education. Portsmouth, NH: Heinemann Press.

Arlow, M. (2004). 'Citizenship Education in a Divided Society' in S. Tawil and A. Harley (2004) Education, Conflict and Social Cohesion. Geneva: UNESCO International Bureau of Education.

Bajaj, M. (2008). "Critical Peace Education." In Encyclopedia of Peace Education, edited by M. Bajaj, 135–146. Charlotte, NC: Information Age Publishing.

Bajaj, M. (2009). "'I Have Big Things Planned for My Future': The Limits and Possibilities of Transformative Agency in Zambian Schools." *Compare* 39(4), 551–568.

Bajaj, M. (2012a). Schooling for Social Change: The Rise and Impact of Human Rights Education in India. New York: Bloomsbury.

Bajaj, M. (2012b). "Human Rights Education in Small Schools in India." *Peace Review* 24(1), 6–13.

Bajaj, M. (2015). Pedagogies of Resistance and Critical Peace Education Praxis. *Journal of Peace Education* 2015 8(2), 154–166.

Bajaj, M. & Brantmeier, E. J. (2011). "Introduction to the Special Issue of the Journal of Peace Education on the Politics." *Possibilities and Praxis of a Critical Peace Education* 8(3), 221–224.

Banks, J. (1999). An Introduction to Multicultural Education. Boston: Allyn and Bacon.

Banks, J. (2008). Educational Researcher, Vol. 37, No. 3, pp. 129–139.

Barton, K. C. (2001). A Picture's Worth. *Social Education* 65(5), 278–283.

Bekerman, Z. (2009). "Identity Versus Peace: Identity Wins." *Harvard Educational Review* 79(1), 74–83.

162 References

Bekerman, Z. & Zembylas. M. (2012). Teaching Contested Narratives: Identity, Memory and Reconciliation in Peace Education and Beyond. Cambridge: Cambridge University Press.

Benhabib, S. (2004). The Rights of Others: Aliens, Residents, and Citizens. Cambridge: Cambridge University Press.

Benhabib, S. (2006). Another Cosmopolitanism. In: R. Post (ed.) Another Cosmopolitanism, with Commentaries by Jeremy Waldron, Bonnie Honig, and Will Kymlicka. Oxford: Oxford University Press, pp. 13–82.

Benhabib, S. (2007). Democratic Exclusions and Democratic Iterations: Dilemmas of 'Just Membership' and Prospects of Cosmopolitan Federalism. *European Journal of Political Theory* 6, 445–462.

Berry, C., Schmied, L. A. & Schrock, J. C. (2008). The Role of Emotion in Teaching and Learning History: A Scholarship of Teaching Exploration. *History Teacher* 41(4), 437–452.

Boulding, E. (1972). A Peace Research: Dialectics and Development. *Journal of Conflict Resolution* 16(4), 469–475. Consortium on Peace Research, Education and Development (COPRED). 1995. Peace Studies Directory. Fairfax, VA: COPRED.

Boulding, E. & Forsberg, R. (1998). Abolishing War: Dialogues with Peace Scholars. Boston Research Center.

Brantmeier, E. J. (2011). "Toward Mainstreaming Critical Peace Education in U.S. Teacher Education." In Critical Pedagogy in the 21st Century: A New Generation of Scholars, edited by C. S. Malott and B. Porfilio, 349–375. Greenwich, CT: Information Age Publishing.

Brantmeier, E. J. & Bajaj, M. (2013). "Peace Education Praxis: Select Resources for Educators and Researchers." In Educating about Social Issues in the 20th and 21st Centuries: A Critical Annotated Bibliography. Vol. 2, e.

Burns, M. (2006). A Thousand Words: Promoting Teachers' Visual Literacy Skills. *Multimedia and Internet at Schools* 13(1), 16–20.

Butler, J. & Mouffe, C. (1997). The Uses of Equality. *Diacritics* 27(1), 3–12.

Callow, J. (2006). Images, Politics, and Multiliteracies: Using a Visual Metalanguage. *Australian Journal of Language and Literacy* 29(1), 7–23.

Castles, S. & Davidson, A. (2000). Citizenship and Migration: Globalization and the Politics of Belonging. New York: Routledge.

Charlie and Ollie Allen [digital image]. Retrieved August 17, 2014, from http://www.loc.gov/pictures/collection/nclc/item/ncl2004001122/PP/.

Chiodo, J. J. & Byford, J. (2004). Do They Really Dislike Social Studies? A Study of Middle School and High School Students. *Journal of Social Studies Research* 28(1), 16–26.

Coventry, M., Felten, P., Jaffee, D., O'Leary, C. & Weis, T. (2006). Ways of Seeing: Evidence and Learning in the History Classroom. *Journal of American History* 92(4), 1371–1402.

Cowhey, M. (2006). Black Ants and Buddhists, Thinking Critically and Teaching Differently in the Primary Grades. Portland, ME: Stenhouse Publishers.

Davies, L. Schools and War: Urgent Agendas for Comparative and International Education in Compare Vol. 35, No. 4, December 2005, pp. 357–371.

Davies, L. (2004). Conflict and Education: Complexity and Chaos. London: RoutledgeFalmer.

Davies, L., Harber, C. & Schweisfurth, M. (2003). Global Review of 50 Years of UNESCO (Associated Schools Birmingham, Centre for International Education and Research).

References **163**

Davies, L., Harber, C. & Yamashita, H. (2004). Global Citizenship: The Needs of Teachers and Learners Report to DFID (Birmingham, Centre for International Education and Research).

Dawes, J. (2007). That the World May Know: Bearing Witness to Atrocity. New York: Harvard University Press.

Delpit, L. (2013). Multiplication is for White People: Raising Expectations for Other People's Children. New York: The New Press.

Dewey, J. (1916). Democracy and Education. New York: Macmillan Press.

Felten, P. (2008). Visual literacy. *Change* 40(6), 60–63.

Freire, P. (1983). The Importance of the Act of Reading. *Journal of Education* 165(1), 5–11.

Freire, P. (1997). Pedagogy of the Oppressed. *Penguin Education* 165(1), 5–11.

Freire, P. (2001). Pedagogy of Freedom: Ethics Democracy and Civic Courage. New York: Rowman & Littlefield.

Freire, P. & Macedo, D. (1987). Literacy Reading the Word and the World. Santa Barbara, CA: Praeger Press.

Gardner, H. (1993). Multiple Intelligences: The Theory in Practice. New York: Basic Books.

Gee, J. P. (2003). What Video Games Have to Teach us About Learning and Literacy. New York: Palgrave Macmillan.

Giroux, H. & Giroux, S. (2004). Take Back Higher Education: Race, Youth, and the Crisis of Democracy in the Post-Civil Rights Era. New York: Palgrave.

Goolkasian, P. (2000). Pictures, Words, and Sounds: From Which Format Are We Best Able to Reason? *The Journal of General Psychology* 127(4), 439–459.

Gounari, P. (2013). Critical Pedagogy and Peace Education: Understanding Violence, Human Rights, and the Historical Project of Militant Peace in Trifonas, P. and Wright B. (2013) Critical Peace Education: Difficult Dialogues. Dordrecht, Heidelberg, New York and London: Springer.

Greene, M. (2005). Teaching in a Moment of Crisis: The Spaces of Imagination. *The New Educator* 1(2), 77–80.

Hamann, S. B., Ely, T. D., Grafton, S. T. & Kilts, C. D. (1999). Amygdala Activity Related to Enhanced Memory for Pleasant and Aversive Stimuli. Nature Neuroscience 2(3), 289–293.

Hammond, L. (2010). The Flat World and Education: How America's Commitment to Equity Will Determine our Future. New York: Teachers College Press.

Hardt, M. & Negri, A. (2004). Multitude War and Democracy in the Age of Empire. New York: Penguin.

Harris, I., Fisk, L., & Rank, C. (1998). A Portrait of University Peace Studies in North America and Western Europe at the End of the Millennium. *International Journal of Peace Studies* 3(1), 91–112.

Harris, I. & Morrison, M. (2012). Peace Education, 3rd Edition. Jefferson, NC: McFarland.

Hess, D. (2009). Controversy in the Classroom: The Democratic Power of Discussion. London and New York: Routledge.

Hine, L. (1908). Dillon (S.C.) Mills. Charley Baxley. Has Doffed 4 Years. Gets 50 Cents. Had Been Out Hunting [digital image]. Retrieved August 17, 2014, from http://www.loc.gov/pictures/collection/nclc/item/ncl2004000507/PP/.

Hine, L. (1908). Doffers in Trenton Mills, Gastonia, N.C. Others as Small and Some Smaller. Little Girls Too [digital image]. Retrieved August 17, 2014 from http://www.loc.gov/pictures/collection/nclc/item/ncl2004000968/PP/ Hine, L. (1913).

164 References

Housing conditions, Floyd Cotton Mill [digital image]. Retrieved August 17, 2014, from http://www.loc.gov/pictures/item/ncl2004002442/PP/ Hine, L. (1914).

Hine, L. (1914). Nannie Coleson, Looper Who Said She Was 11 Years Old, and Has Been Working in the Crescent Hosiery Mill for Some Months [digital image]. Retrieved August 17, 2014, from http://www.loc.gov/pictures/collection/nclc/item/ncl2004004146/PP/.

Hootstein, E. W. (1995). Motivational Strategies of Middle School Social Studies Teachers. *Social Education* 59(1), 23–26.

hooks, b. (2000). Where We Stand, Class Matters. New York: Routledge.

Hopgood, S. (2015). The End Times of Human Rights. Ithaca, NY: Cornell University Press.

JanMohamed, A. (1987). Toward a Theory of Minority Discourse in Cultural Critique 6, pp. 5–11.

Jaramillo, N. & Carreon, M. (2014). Pedagogies of Resistance and Solidarity: Towards Revolutionary and Decolonial Praxis. *Interface* 6(1), 392–411.

Kensinger, E. A. & Corkin, S. (2003). Memory Enhancement for Emotional Words: Are Emotional Words More Vividly Remembered Than Neutral Words? *Memory and Cognition* 31(8), 1169–1180.

Laclau E. & Mouffe, C. (2001). Hegemony and Socialist Strategy: Towards a Radical Democratic Politics. New York: Verso.

Ladson-Billings, G. (2004). "Culture Versus Citizenship: The Challenge of Racialized Citizenship in the United States." James A. Banks (ed.), Diversity and Citizenship Education. San Francisco: Jossey-Bass/Wiley.

Lange, M. (2012). Educations in Ethnic Violence. Cambridge: Cambridge University Press.

Leming, J. (1992). "The Influence of Contemporary Issues Curricula on School-Aged Youth." Review of Research in Education. Vol. 18. pp. 111–161.

Levine, L. J. & Pizarro, D. A. (2004). Emotion and Memory Research: A Grumpy Overview. Social Cognition 22(5), 530–554. doi:10.1521/soco.22.5.530.50767 Ohio Social Studies Review, Fall 2014, Volume 51, Issue 2 22.

Levine, R. M. (2004). Insights into American History: Photographs as Documents. Saddleback, NJ: Pearson/Prentice Hall.

Little, D., Felten, P. & Berry, C. (2010). Liberal Education in a Visual World. *Liberal Education* 96(2), 44–49.

Madison, J. H. (2004). Teaching With Images. *OAH Magazine of History* 18(2), 65–68.

Maira, S. (2005). "The Intimate and the Imperial: South Asian Muslim Immigrant Youth After 9/11." Sunaina Maira and Elisabeth Soep (eds.), Youthscapes: The Popular, the National, the Global. Philadelphia: University of Pennsylvania Press, pp. 64–84.

McCarthy, C. (1998). The Uses of Culture Education and the Limits of Ethnic Affiliation. New York and London: Routledge.

Mills, G. E. (2003). Action Research: A Guide for the Teacher Researcher, 2nd Ed. Upper Saddle River, NJ: Prentice Hall.

Nieto, S. (1999). The Light in Their Eyes Creating Multicultural Learning Communities. New York: Teachers College Press.

Nussbaum, M. (2002). Patriotism and Cosmopolitanism. In J. Cohen (Ed.), For Love of Country (pp. 2–17). Boston: Beacon.

O'Hare, P. (1983). Education for Peace and Justice. San Francisco: Harper & Row.

Perugini, N. & Gordon, N. (2015). The Human Right to Dominate. Oxford: Oxford University Press.

Reardon, B. (1988). Comprehensive Peace Education. Educating for Global Responsibility. New York: Teachers College Press.

Reardon, B. (1988b). Educating for Global Responsibility: Teacher Designed Curricula for Peace Education. New York: Teachers College Press.

Reardon, B. (2013). Meditating on the Barricades: Concerns, Cautions and Possibilities for Peace Education for Political Efficacy in Trifonas and Wright Critical Peace Education Difficult Dialogues. London and New York: Springer.

Reason, C. & Reason, L. (2007). Asking the Right Questions. *Educational Leadership* 65(1), 36–40.

Rideout, V. (2013). Zero to Eight: Children's Media Use in America 2013. Common Sense Media. Retrieved from http://www.commonsensemedia.org/research.

Rorty, R. (1989). Contingency, Irony, and Solidarity. Cambridge: Cambridge University Press.

Rosaldo, R. (1997). Cultural Citizenship, Inequality, and Multiculturalism. In W. V. Flores & R. Benmayor (Eds.), Latino Cultural Citizenship: Claiming Identity, Space, and Rights (pp. 27–28). Boston: Beacon.

Russell, W. B. & Waters, S. (2010). Instructional Methods for Teaching Social Studies: A Survey of What Middle School Students Like and Dislike About Social Studies Instruction. *Journal for the Liberal Arts and Sciences* 14(2), 7–14.

Samaras, A. & Freese, A. (2006). Self-study of Teaching Practices: A Primer. New York: Peter Lang.

Segall, A. (1999). Critical History: Implications for History/Social Studies Education. *Theory and Research in Social Education* 27(3).

Segall, A., Heilman, E. E. & Cherryholmes, C. H. (Eds.) (2006). *Social Studies – the Next Generation: Re-searching in the Postmodern.* New York: Peter Lang.

Shaughnessy, J. M. & Haladyna, T. M. (1985). Research on Student Attitude Toward Social Studies. *Social Education* 49(8), 692–95.

Torres, C., Olmos, L. & Heertum, R. (2006). In the Shadow of Neoliberalism: Thirty Years of Educational Reform in North America. Dubai: Bentham Books.

Trifonas, P. & Wright, B. (2013). Critical Peace Education: Difficult Dialogues. London and New York: Springer.

Trump doctrine takes shape with more divisive talk - MRT.com: Our View Editorials. Retrieved October 2016, from http://www.mrt.com/opinion/our_view_editorials/article_1e612a68–9e18–11e5-b207–7bfc460503e9.html#ixzz3tq1Fe1In.

Verma, R. (2005). Dialogues About 9/11, the Media, and Race: Lessons from a Secondary Classroom. *Radical Teacher,* Issue 74 (pp. 12–15).

Verma, R. (2008). Backlash: South Asian Immigrant Voices on the Margins. Dordrecht, Netherlands: Sense Publishers. Foreword by Dr. Michael Apple.

Verma, R. (2010). Be the Change: Teacher Activist Global Citizen. Bern Switzerland: Peter Lang Publishing.

Verma, R. (2012). Between Spaces of Otherness and Belonging in Democratic Citizenship in Schools: Teaching Controversial Issues, Traditions and Accountability. London: Dunedin Academic Press.

Vigil, J. (1988). Barrio Gangs: Street Life and Identity in Southern California. Austin, TX: University of Texas Press.

Waters, S. & Russell, W. B. (2012). Visual Literacy Strategies for the Social Studies Classroom. In Teaching and Learning Social Studies: Integrative Strategies for the K-12 Social Studies Classroom (pp. 209–224). Greenwich, CT: Information Age Publishing.

Werner, W. (2002). Reading Visual Texts. *Theory and Research in Social Education* 30(3), 401–428.

Whitehead, J. (2000). How do I Improve my Practice? Creating and Legitimating an Epistemology of Practice. *Reflective Practice* 1(1), 91–104.

Woyshner, C. (2006). Picturing Women: Gender, Images, and Representation. *Social Education* 70(6), 358–362.

Yoshino, K. (2007) Covering: The Hidden Assault on Our Civil Rights. Random House.

Young, I. M. (1989). Polity and Group Difference: A Critique of the Ideal of Universal Citizenship. *Ethics* 99(2), 250–274.

Young, I. M. (2000). Inclusion and Democracy. New York: Oxford University Press.

Zull, J. E. (2004). The Art of Changing the Brain. *Educational Leadership* 62(1), 68–72.

INDEX

action research 12, 82
activist 11; identities 53–55; peace 2, 5,
 28–35, 44–45, 54, 147; teacher as 3, 5,
 34–35, 79–82, 97–113
Afghan Peace Volunteers 97–98
agents of change 32
AJK Diversified 13
American-Arab Anti-Discrimination
 League 25
anti-immigrant sentiment 17, 25, 26, 89,
 90, 93–94
apartheid 49, 50
Appiah, K. A. 154
Apple, Michael 11, 34, 39, 53, 155
Arab-American Anti-Discrimination
 Committee 7
Argueta, Sergio 123–5
Arlow, M. 50

Bajaj, Monisha 20, 22
Banks, James 39
Bekerman, Zvi 18–19, 54
belonging and Otherness 23
Benhabib, S. 16, 23, 24, 69
Black Lives Matter 21, 60, 90, 94
Blue Lives Matter 21, 60
Boko Haram 10, 61, 147, 149
boys, sex trafficking of 2, 157–8
Brantmeier, Edward 79, 156–7
Brexit initiative 17, 24–25
Bring Back Our Girls movement 147–9
Brown, Michael 21

Brown *vs.* Board of Education 77
bullying 13, 65, 66, 67–77; and genocide
 70–73

Carreon, M. 20
Castellano, Bruce 102–13
Chavez, Cesar 51–53
children, sex trafficking of 1–2, 157–8
citizenship: global 16–17, 22–33, 153–5;
 reconfiguration of 24
Claire Friedlander Education Institute 73
Clemente, Roberto 41–42, 44–46
Clements, Robert 38
collective identities, mobilization
 around 21
commodification of bodies 1, 3
common core curriculum 12, 36–55;
 examples of unofficial lessons 41–46
Comunidad y Vida program 119–20
cooperative learning 4–5, 9
cosmopolitanism 154
Cowhey, Mary 37
critical design experts 54
culture of power 23
curriculum 127–8; common core 12,
 36–55; making more inclusive 39–40;
 transformation paradigm in 40;
 unofficial 33–35, 41–46

Davies, L. 26–27
Dawes, James 99
Defense of Marriage Act (DOMA) 94

168 Index

dehumanization 1, 2, 3, 5, 8, 80–83, 94, 116, 134–6, 147, 149, 153, 160
Delpit, Lisa 152
Dewey, John 9
diasporic identities 23–24
Dignity for All Students Act (DASA Act) 13, 63, 66–77
discrimination, covering up 110–11
Dream Act Dreamers 21

Education Action Group (EAG) 38–39
elementary classroom and peace education 36–55
End Times of Human Rights (Hopgood) 146
ethnocentrism 153

Farris, Christine King 47
fear *versus* peace discussion 89–93
Felten, P. 57
female gang members 115–16
Freire, Paulo 9, 79, 80, 83, 115–16, 132, 156

gangs: creating awareness about 122–5; prevention policies 116–17
gang shakeup 116–17
Garrison-Feinberg, Tracy 73
genocide and bullying 70–73
girls, sex trafficking of 1–2, 157–8
Giroux, Henry 41
Giroux, Susan 41
global citizenship 22–27, 97–99; education 153–5; as interruptive democracy 26–27; rejection of 16–17; shaping 28–33
globalization 22–23, 153
Gordon, N. 28, 32
Gounari, Panayota 19–20
Graythen, Chris 131
Greene, Maxine 14–15, 157

Hammond, Linda Darling 152
Harris, Ian 17–18, 126–7
Harvesting Hope: The Story of Cesar Chavez (Krull) 39, 51
hate crimes 7, 25, 65, 67, 75–77, 111
Hernandez, Daniel 68
Hess, Diana 101
Hitler, Adolf 92
Holocaust 71–74, 92

Holocaust Memorial and Tolerance Center 13, 70–74
homelessness 60–63
homophobia 111–12
hooks, bell 82
Hopgood, Stephen 146
Huckabee, Mike 93
Hughes, Langston 47
humanization of teachers 81–82, 87
human rights 14, 24, 27–28, 50–53, 127, 146–7, 153; universal 128–31
human trafficking 1–2
Hurricane Katrina 131–2

"I am a Man" photograph 58
images used in peace education 57–63
immigrants, victimization of 17, 25, 26, 89
immigration narratives 136–40
Increase the Peace program 106–13
International Decade for a Culture of Peace and Non-Violence for the Children of the World 96
interruptive democracy 24, 54; definition 22
Islamophobia 7, 25, 30, 67, 75, 97

The Jacket (Clements) 38–39
Jacobson, Aileen 73
Jaramillo, N. 20

Keneth, Alisty Joy 74–77
King, Martin Luther, Jr. 46–50
Krull, Kathleen 39, 51
Kure, Natu Suzie 147–9

learner-actor-activist 121, 147
learner-actors 22, 34
learning, cooperative 4–5, 9
Leming, James 32
Le Pen, Jean Marine 159
LGBT community 25, 66, 111–12; rights 94, 109–10
Lilach, Beth 70–73
Lingenfelter, Sue 1, 2, 157–8
Love146, 1
Lucero, Marcelo 65

Mandela, Nelson 47, 48–49
Martin, Dave 131
Martin, Trayvon 91
media: consciousness and stereotypes 131–3; political and oppression 134–40
Mendoza, Carlos 22

mentors in schools 120–1
middle school classroom and peace education 56–63
model minority stereotype 75
mondialisation 23
Morris, Rob 1, 2
Morrison, Mary Lee 17–18
Muslim Alliance for Sexual and Gender Diversity 112
Muslim community preventing hate crimes 7, 25, 110
My Brother Martin: A Sister Remembers Growing up with Rev. Martin Luther King Jr. (Farris) 47

Nassau County Anti-Bias Task Force 108–9
nationalism 153
nationalist imaginaries 69
nationhood, politics of 24
nation-states, belonging to 24–25, 69
"New Right" movement 102, 103
Nieto, Soonia 40
Nussbaum, M. 154

oppression and political media 134–40
Orlando Florida gay nightclub shooting 14, 111–12
Otherness 69; and belonging 23

Pannu, Karanveer Singh 68
Paris terrorist attacks in 2015, 29–32, 66, 67, 90, 143, 146
peace, defining and redefining 8
peace activism, defining 17–22
peace activists 44–45, 54, 147; shaping 28–33; teacher as 2, 5, 34–35, 79–82, 97–113
peace education 3, 4; in the elementary classroom's common core curriculum 36–55; incorporating into schools 8–11; as inquiry-based endeavor 22; interrupting violence 115; mainstreaming 156–7; making meaning through lived experiences 7–8; memorializing 9/11 terrorist attack on the World Trade Center 7–8; in middle school classroom 56–63; public schools' struggle to engage and dialogue about peace education 17–18; as relational encounters between teacher and learner 16–19; stages of 79; training

teachers in 78–100; unofficial lessons on race 40–55
peaceful protest 6
peace pedagogy 11, 13, 17, 20–21, 37, 41, 62, 78–100
peace praxis 10, 12, 95
pedagogies of resistance 19–20
Perugini, N. 28, 32
political media and oppression 134–40
politics of nationhood 24
power 34; complicit to 32; culture of 23, 34; and oppression 39–40

race, unofficial lessons on 41–46
racial profiling 134–6
racism 7, 42–50
racist nativism 7, 9, 17, 22, 24, 97
Reardon, Betty 18
reflection in teacher education 82
refugee camps 62
refugees, misunderstanding and criminalizing of 140–3
Rito, J. Jill 96–99
Roberto Clemente: Pride of the Pittsburgh Pirates (Winter) 41–42
Rosaldo, R. 155

school climate 13, 66
schools: incorporating peace education into 8–11; not supporting at-risk youth 119–21; peace education in elementary school 36–55; peace education in middle school 56–63; reinforcing conformity 8–9; unofficial curriculum in 33–35, 41–46
segregation 47, 58, 65, 86
self-identity in gangs 116
self-study 82
sex tourists 1–2
sex trade 1–2, 157–8
Seymour, David 60
Sikh Coalition 7, 25
Sikh community 7, 110
Social Action Approach to education 39–40
social media responding to violence 29–31
social movements 21
Soledad as a case study of at-risk youth succeeding 114–25
Southern Poverty Law Center 69
stereotypes and media consciousness 131–3
stereotyping 7

170 Index

S.T.R.O.N.G. organization 123–5
Students United 97
subjective violence 19
symbolic violence 83–87, 132–3
Syrian refugee crisis 140–9; as a lesson
  88–89, 93–94

teacher: emerging as a student 5;
  humanization of 81–82, 87; training
  peace education practices 13, 78–100
teacher activists 3, 5, 34–35, 81–82, 97–100;
  case study 101–13; educating to be 79–80
teacher education: connecting teachers
  globally 95–96; global crises as everyday
  lessons 88–93; peace pedagogies for
  78–100; understanding symbolic
  violence 83–87
teacher educators 13
Teach for America program 114
teaching, banking method of 79
TED Talks 136–40
"*Tereska Draws her Home*" (photograph) 60
terrorism, memorialization of 7–8
9/11 terrorist attack on the World Trade
  Center: memorialized in education 7–8;
  prompting nativism 68, 75, 91, 97, 101
testing opt-out movement 150–2
Torres, C. 23
transformation paradigm in education 40
Trump, Donald 21, 25, 49, 68, 70, 92,
  134, 159
Trump Doctrine 25
Trump Effect 68–69

United Nations conference on Teaching
  Peace and Human Rights 95–96
United Nations Declaration on Human
  Rights 27
Universal Declaration of Human Rights
  94, 153

Verma, Parveen 116–17, 119, 122
Vigil, James Diego 116
violence: acknowledging 10; becoming
  normalized 20, 41; interpretations of
  in the middle school classroom 56–63;
  interrupted by peace education 115;
  prevalence of 14, 16; responding to
  29–32; in schools 64–77; solidarity
  against 29–30; subjective 19; symbolic
  132–3; symbolic shaping teachers
  83–87

white privilege 38, 81
Wilson, Darren 21
Winter, Jonah 41
Withers, Ernest 58
workers' rights 53
World Teach program 99

Yoshino, Kenji 110–11
Young Conservatives 38–39
youth, at-risk 114–25

Zembylas, Michalinos 18–19, 54
Zimmerman, George 91
Zootopia (movie) 90–92